SEASONS OF REMEMBRANCE

ONE FAMILY'S HERITAGE

William Furman

authorHOUSE®

AuthorHouse™
1663 Liberty Drive
Bloomington, IN 47403
www.authorhouse.com
Phone: 833-262-8899

Published by AuthorHouse 09/21/2021

ISBN: 978-1-4389-9250-1 (sc)
ISBN: 978-1-4389-9251-8 (hc)

Print information available on the last page.

ACKNOWLEDGMENTS

Without the help and support of the two most important women in my life this book would never have been written. A special thank you to Barbara Furman and Donna LeNarz.

I also want to thank Chuck Kiefer and Linden Swift for encouraging me to write this story.

The following people shared stories and letters that provided information. They too have my gratitude.

Kathleen Cushing
Jessie Chambers (deceased)
Larry DeWitt
Rodney Furman
Evelyn Vincent
Gladys Sailor (deceased)
Other sources of information:
Sheridan County Historical Museum
Sheridan County records
Wicks Genealogy Record

PREFACE

Did you ever wonder how large tracts of land were developed into ranches? Did you ever wonder who were the people that developed them?

This is the story of an actual family who planted roots on the Nebraska prairie. In over a 50-year period they developed a 160-acre homestead into a ranch of more than 7,000 acres with a successful cattle-raising operation. Many of the accounts you will read are true. Others are what might have been.

I am a descendant of this family. When thoughts of Nebraska come to my mind, I see a blue sky with puffy clouds extending from horizon to horizon. Sometimes at sunset rain can be seen falling which changes its downward course when caught by the wind. Below, the ground is an ocean of brown grass that waves like the sea. Looking out beyond the rolling hills, one can see forever. And, at sunset, the sky is full of vivid colors: red, orange, and yellow. Nowhere else can such a sunset be seen.

Standing on a prairie hill as a young boy, I became aware that some great powerful being must have created this wide expanse and I realize just how small I am compared to what surrounds me and that great powerful being. My roots are there.

A TIME FOR EVERYTHING

There is a time for everything,
And a season for every activity under heaven.

A time to be born and a time to die,
A time to plant and a time to uproot,
A time to kill and a time to heal,
A time to tear down and a time to build,
A time to weep and a time to laugh,
A time to mourn and a time to dance,
A time to scatter stones and a time to gather them,
A time to embrace and a time to refrain,
A time to search and a time to give up,
A time to keep and a time to throw away,
A time to tear and a time to mend,
A time to be silent and a time to speak
A time to love and a time to hate,
A time for war and a time for peace.

Ecclesiastes 3:1-8

CHAPTER 1
A TIME TO SEARCH

The love of Nebraska seed was planted in the fall of 1886 when my great grandfather, James L. Furman, went to Nebraska in search of open land. James was a 27-year-old man who used few words but had the voice of a giant. He stood just less than six feet tall. Hard work throughout his youth had made him strong. Married two years earlier, he taught school to supplement his income from farming. He had left his wife of 15 months back in Iowa. It was not to be a permanent arrangement. James had read the enticing advertisements by the railroads of available land in western Nebraska through the Homestead program.

Iowa had obtained statehood 40 years earlier. The Indians had been pushed out of the territory. Farms of all sizes covered the green rolling hills of the state. The state boasted of a population over 1,500,000 people. James felt confined and limited by Iowa's advancement.

With the open land gone in Iowa, James saw an opportunity to own his own farm. The Homestead Act made land in Nebraska available. This allowed, for a $10 filing fee and living on the staked land for five years, a person to obtain ownership to a quarter section of land.

After going over this in his mind for several days, finally James said to his wife, "Belle, just think about the opportunity to own an entire quarter section of land. We could in Nebraska."

"James, what are you talking about?"

"Here we do not have the money to buy 20 acres of land, let alone 160 acres, but in Nebraska we can own 160 acres for just $10! Whenever there is any land for sale here, it takes a lot of money to buy it."

Helen Isabelle was his wife's full name but everybody called her Belle. Belle was by nature a true lady. She was short in stature, of strong character, and a sensitive individual. She loved to read to children and would laugh and cry as much as the children who listened. She was quick to minister to neighbors and friends in illness and trouble.

Belle responded, "Nebraska! I have heard there are Indians causing trouble out there. I don't care if the Sioux are living on reservations now, they could kill us! And railroads are not in existence in western Nebraska. Towns there are not even civilized. How could people have any social life? Besides all that, we would be leaving both of our families if we moved there. Forget that idea, James."

"Belle, do you remember not long ago how the grasshoppers wiped out most crops in Iowa and how people struggled to have enough food to eat? It could happen again. There are other things that could go wrong and I am farming jointly with my family; if something should happen, we would never gain anything. While in Nebraska there had been reports of good rainfalls, which produced above average crops. And as for Indians, they have not caused any problems for five years." After more discussion, James finally convinced Belle that a great opportunity as well as an adventure was open to them in Nebraska.

"James, you will never be satisfied until you find out about this, so go see the land. But if it does not look promising, then promise me you will return home and forget the homestead idea." This was difficult for Belle to say because she was expecting their first child.

James wanted to look Nebraska over before the snows came, and in his thinking Belle would be well cared for by family and a good doctor if he did not get back in time. So James boarded a train for the first time in his life and headed west. His thoughts went back to his young boyhood days when his father and mother migrated to Iowa from Pennsylvania. Although he did not remember very much since he was only seven years old when they settled in Iowa, that trip had been made by horse and wagon and took months.

The first stop was Webster City, Iowa where he changed trains to Sioux City, then crossed the Missouri River, and his last leg of the journey was to Valentine, Nebraska. The railroad did continue on, but the land office was in Valentine. This would be the place to ask questions and gain information, so it made sense to stop here.

James found he was not the only man in town interested in free land. A few other interested men had come to Valentine seeking the same information as he. There was a lot of talk about homesteading and how things worked. James spent several hours looking at maps at the land office that showed available land. Most of the land in the eastern part of the state had been claimed. The available land was in the northwest part of the state.

One other thing he learned was the name of a man, Jules Sandoz. Jules was said to know more about available land and homesteading than anyone else in the state. It was also said that he was a very "odd duck". But he had helped others start a homestead claim. The word was that he came to Valentine this time of year. So James waited and a few days later Jules Sandoz showed up.

All that had been said about Jules was true. He was different but seemed to be knowledgeable. James felt this man could be of great help. The offer of a free meal and a glass of whiskey was all that was necessary to get Jules to tell all about western Nebraska. Jules really enticed James with all his glowing reports of the sand hills of Nebraska.

The next day James found out he had provided the local men a good laugh by buying Jules supper and whiskey. They told him Jules talks all the time about sand hill country and how everybody should go there. But James did not mind. To him it had all been worthwhile.

To Jules the sand hills of Nebraska were as close to heaven as one could get. He encouraged everybody to move to western Nebraska. Jules was planning to return to his home as soon as he took care of some business and said he would show James some available land if he wanted to make the trip. James couldn't wait. He spent a restless time waiting for Jules to leave.

While James was in Valentine, Belle was with her family, but she missed James. She was no longer teaching piano lessons and she was expecting. She had time on her hands and very little to do. She was lonely. Sunday was the one day she felt good because she played the piano at church and there was usually a lot of socializing after the morning service.

Three days later Jules, James and Thomas Preston, who was also interested in a homestead claim, were on the train headed for a town called Rushville. That night they rented a room above the saloon; all three slept in the room. The next morning Jules picked up his horse from a friend and gathered mail from the post office. It seemed everyone knew Jules. James and Thomas Preston rented horses to ride across the prairie with Jules searching for land to homestead. They started out under a clear sky with a cool breeze. As they left Rushville, James remarked to Thomas, "You can see forever."

Jules was headed to his place but would get home by a circuitous route. He had mail to deliver since he was considered a postmaster in the area. Besides there were two men interested in homesteading who were riding with him and they needed to see the land.

James and Thomas spent the day riding through the hills with Jules. Each time they stopped at a homestead to leave mail, James found friendly families and had offers of food from all of them. The people and the openness of the land appealed to James. He felt so free with nothing to hinder him from anything.

When darkness began to fall, James and Thomas decided they should return to Rushville. "You fellers think you can find your way back to town?"

"If you start us in the right direction, we will find it OK."

Jules pointed them in the right direction and told them of landmarks to look for to find their way back to town. "Rushville is northwest from here. Watch for blowouts, that way you will always know you are going northwest."

"What are blowouts?"

"Blowouts are cupped out places on the northwest side of hills, usually on the upper slope. The winter winds form a pocket in the sand.

Keep going northwest and you should find Rushville." Jules continued his way homeward. They parted with Jules, promising to help file a claim and get them started with a homestead if they decided to stay.

The next morning both men started out again, this time alone. Thomas wanted to go north and James went south toward the Niobrara River. He had ridden for more than half the day when he came to a bluff with a river at the bottom. As he sat there on his horse, looking out at the low hills covered in blowing grass, the gentle wind seemed to be saying, "There across the river is your home."

Yes, he thought this is the right place. He could not wait to tell Belle! But first he must find Jules. He had a million questions. Back to town he headed. He needed to know how to find Jules. Time was important now since some snow was on the ground; fall was turning into winter. The change in seasons could not be missed because of the large V formations of geese going south. If a person could not see them, he could hear them.

The following morning, James, full of excitement, headed deeper into the sand hills looking for Jules. After some trial and error he came upon what looked like half a home on the side of a hill. There were sod blocks about 18 inches by 10 inches stacked from the hillside and the front was made of sod blocks and rough sawn boards. There was one window in front. The rest of the home was a dugout back into the hillside.

This was Jules' place. A tired looking woman came out when James called, "Hello. Is Jules here?"

"No, he is out hunting and I have no idea when or if he will be back. He goes and comes when he wants. You can stay and wait for him to return if you want. Might be a long wait." Looking around and being told Jules might be gone for days, James decided to return to Rushville.

"My name is James Furman. Would you tell Jules that I want to talk to him about filing a claim? I found where I want to live."

Back in town, he wrote Belle that he had found a good place for them and he would return after filing a claim. He described the land, the sky, and the river in words of splendor. He thought he had better not say just yet that it was 12 miles out of town. Instead he described Rushville as a town with permanent buildings; it had several stores and a school; it even had a church. He hoped Belle would like it as much as he did.

Then he waited for Jules to show up. Every day he would ride out to the river and plan. Although the rides would be cold, the snows had been light. So many thoughts went through his mind. How would he get enough wood to build a house? Should he build a sod house like he had seen in other places? Where would be the best ground for planting crops?

A week later Jules came into Rushville. James bombarded him with questions. James asked, "Has anyone filed a claim on his chosen land? Should he worry about someone else filing on the same land? Would Jules help him stake it out? Who could he get to survey the land? What papers needed to be filled out and where do you get the proper papers?"

Jules listened for awhile and said, "You worry too much. I have already done most of the surveying in the area and we just need to locate the corner stakes and write down the coordinates. For three bottles of whiskey I'll help you do what you need to do." So for the next two days Jules and James located the corner stakes and resurveyed the land. James recorded on paper the boundaries by longitude and latitude as Jules instructed.

James took the next morning train back to Valentine to file his claim. He planned to continue on back to his home in Iowa after filing. He wanted to be there for the birth of his first child. At the land office, he was surprised to learn that if he filed, he was expected to return immediately to the claim and start setting up a home. James was at a loss as to what to do. He had told Belle he was on the way back and to expect him home in a few days. Now what should he do?

Would someone else claim the land before he could return? James walked out of that office a dejected man and spent a worried night over what he should do. The next morning his decision was to return to Belle. This was what was most important. He had given his word to return and the baby was due any time now.

Before he got on the train, he did two things. First, he went to the land office and asked the clerk, "Is there any exception to the requirement to return immediately to the filed claim? Would it be possible to return to the homestead in two or three months rather than immediately?"

After some hesitation the clerk said, "A person could be gone from the claim for no more than six months if there was good reason."

"Mister, I have two good reasons. First, my wife is about to give birth to our first child and, second, I need to go back to Iowa to get tools and goods to start a homestead." The clerk hesitated but agreed to file a claim in James' name.

[4—063.]

HOMESTEAD.

Land Office at *Valentine Neb*

Nov 19, 188 6

I, *James L. Furman as Rushville Neb*

having filed my application, No. *7100*, for an entry under Section No. 2289, Revised Statutes of the United States, do solemnly swear that *I am a married man over 21 years of age and a native born citizen of the United States*

that said application, No. *7100*, is made for the purpose of actual settlement and cultivation; that said entry is made for my own exclusive benefit, and not directly or indirectly for the benefit or use of any other person or persons whomsoever; and that I have not heretofore had the benefit of the homestead laws.

X *James L. Furman*

Sworn to and subscribed this *19* day

of *Nov 1886*, before

S. F. Smith

Reg of the Land Office.

NOTE.—If this affidavit be acknowledged before the Clerk of the Court, as provided for by Sec. 2294, U. S. Revised Statutes, the Homestead party must expressly state herein that he or some member of his family is residing upon the land applied for, and that *bona fide* improvement and settlement have been made. He must also state why he is unable to appear at the Land Office.

ELECTRO'S. [2066—30 M.]

homestead paper

8

[4—007.]

HOMESTEAD.

APPLICATION
No. *7100*

Land Office at *Valentine Neb*

Nov. 19, 188 *6*

James L. Furman of *Rushville Neb* , do hereby apply to enter, under Section 2289, Revised Statutes of the United States, the *Lots 3 & 4 & S* *½ NW ¼* of Section *1* , in Township *30* of Range *43* , containing *155.41* acres.

✕ *James L. Furman*

Land Office at *Valentine Neb*

Nov 19th 1886

I, *S. F. Bartch* , REGISTER OF THE LAND OFFICE, do hereby certify that the above application is for *Surveyed Lands* of the class which the applicant is legally entitled to enter under Section 2289, Revised Statutes of the United States, and that there is no prior valid adverse right to the same.

S. F. Bartch

Register.

(2515—30,000.)

homestead paper

Then James wrote to Jules telling about his wife, who was due to deliver their first child and he was going back to her. But he so wanted the place they had staked out and he had filed a claim in Valentine. Could Jules do anything to hold it for him until he could return? He must keep his word to Belle; still he longed to own the land he had seen.

He hoped and prayed that everything would work out. James tried to think about Belle and the new baby all the way back but many times his mind pictured the river and open land. Finally he was back and just in time, for Belle went into labor the very next morning. Thanks to a doctor, a healthy girl was born. Belle was weak but James was full of life and pride.

Things returned to normal for the next few weeks with James working on the family farm with his brothers. Belle was recovering well from the birth, and the baby, Edna, was growing. Everyday James would talk about western Nebraska and the opportunity that was available there. His brothers got tired of listening to him but they did ask if he had seen any buffalos. Surprisingly, his mother seemed the most interested person in the family.

Belle could tell James had his mind set on moving to Nebraska. She did not share his excitement but was married to him for better or worse. She would go, if that was what was to be.

In early spring James received a letter from Jules, which informed him that no one had tried to settle on his claim. However, other people were beginning to file claims in the area. Winter was about over and the leaves were beginning to bud on the trees. James worried that someone else might get "his" land.

After much discussion with Belle, they decided James would go by himself and establish a home. Belle and their daughter would come later, after he got things established. This would give both mother and daughter the chance to grow stronger.

Before he left, James got a shock. On his last night, during supper, his mother remarked, "I just might make a trip out to Nebraska, too! I am tired of Iowa and the neighbors." She had good neighbors; any problems that existed were due to his mother, Mary Pearl. She was a cantankerous person that changed moods often.

On the morning of departure Mary Pearl was nowhere to be found. James loaded the wagon with what he thought would be needed. When it was time to go, he stood with his arms around Belle, who was holding Edna. Neither said anything for awhile. Holding back tears, Belle finally said, "You had better go or you'll miss the train." In her mind was the nagging question of what the future would be like.

James kissed both Belle and Edna and climbed up into the wagon. James' brother, Elmer, drove the wagon to the train. James boarded the train. This separation would be longer and harder on Belle than James, who was somewhat of a loner and didn't seem to need people as much as Belle.

James took much more with him this time. Clothing, cooking utensils, and basic tools were all piled around him in the immigrant car. James had trouble controlling his emotions. He missed Belle and Edna already. And he also wondered what the future held; yet he was excited about the prospect of owning land. He quietly prayed, "God keep my family well and protected, and me, too." The train took him to Webster where he changed trains again and traveled on to Sioux City. Here he would make different travel plans.

James thought the farther west I go the more expensive animals and equipment are going to be. To him it made sense to buy most of what would be needed in Sioux City. James spent much of their savings on two horses and a wagon, as well as a bed, table and chair, and some other necessities for housekeeping.

From Sioux City he headed west toward Valentine. He thought if all went well he could get to Valentine in 10 days or less. There he would stop at the land office to prove he had not been gone for more than six months. The trip went well and at the homes where he stopped for water or rest he found friendly people. Many offered advice and encouragement. But nights of sleeping under the wagon were different than what he was used to. He began to realize many things would be different from now on.

Arriving in Valentine, he went to the land office and found a different clerk. "Hello, I am James Furman, who filed a claim five months ago and will be on my claim before the six months absence period is over." The clerk seemed unconcerned how long he had been gone. "I have too much other work to do besides being concerned about one man's situation."

"I just wanted to make official notice that I have abided the law." The clerk agreed to make note of James' return in the record. James never felt anything would become of his effort to do the right thing but his conscience was clear. After leaving the claims clerk, James decided to spend 50 cents on one night in the hotel and another 50 cents for a meal cooked by someone else. He was tired of his own cooking already.

The following morning he inquired about the prices of crop seed. He thought here it should be cheaper than in Rushville. He bought corn and wheat seed. There was still money left and he thought a cow would be a good idea. After some bargaining he was successful; one milk cow was added to his worldly goods. Next goal was Rushville, another five or six days away. He would start at sunrise.

James found the going slower because of the cow. It might take longer to reach Rushville than he thought. This bothered him but as he drove on, he was pleased with himself. He thought to himself: "I am not yet 30 and Belle and I are on the way to owning 160 acres. In the wagon there is seed for crops and enough household things to begin a home. It is spring 1887 and the future looks good."

Then as the sun climbed through the clouds, worries began to creep into his mind. He thought, "It will be May before I reach Rushville and soon seed would need to be planted. But how? I do not have a plow or a disc. If I buy a plow and disc, I will not have enough money for anything else. Have I made a mistake by buying a cow rather than a plow? What was I thinking? I had my mind on Edna thinking about how she should have milk. She won't even be here for awhile. I need a plow now!"

Also, what about some kind of house? He wanted his family with him and that meant a house. He quickly decided the house would have to wait until the seed was planted. He needed help to plant seed.

The third day out from Valentine, James came upon a family whose wagon had a broken wheel. "Hello, looks like you folks have a problem. Need a hand? My name is James Furman."

"We sure could use some help. We are Bill and Mary Jansen. We are on our way to our new homestead southeast of Rushville." A new friendship was formed that day. In open country no one walked away from someone in need of help. James was not going to do so either. "Bill, can the two of us fix that wheel and remount it?"

"I feel pretty good about the remounting part but a wheelwright may be needed to fix the blamed thing." The two men tried to repair the wheel but realized they could not without the proper tools. A wheelwright was needed and the closest town was Gordon. "James, would you mind taking this wheel to town to get it fixed and bring it back? I just can't leave my wife out here alone."

Neither could Bill leave his wife with a man he had just met. It only made sense for James to take the wheel to Gordon. "Do you have a saddle I could use? I could make better time on one horse."

"I sure do and you can use one of our horses if you want." James unhitched his horses and would ride one of his own. He saddled the horse and after tying the wheel to the saddle horn he rode toward Gordon.

It was dark by the time James returned with a repaired wheel. As the men remounted the wheel on the axle by the light of the camp fire, Mary prepared supper. After eating, the three told about their families, where they were from, and their plans for their new homes. James was thrilled to learn Bill had a plow and suggested they help one another get seed planted – if their claims were close enough for them to work together.

As he crawled into his bedroll that night, James was full of optimism. He was thankful he had met someone who would be a neighbor and a friend – even though they might not live very close to one another. He was tired but sleep did not quiet his mind just yet. There were many thoughts and ideas occupying his brain. Finally, he closed his eyes.

CHAPTER 2
A TIME TO PLANT

A ll three were awake by sunrise.

"Mary, those biscuits were the best I've had since I left Belle. And the coffee sure hit the spot. I'm not much of a cook. A woman does much better than a man."

"Why, thank you James."

After they ate, no time was lost in packing up and harnessing the horses; they were anxious to start. Soon they were going through Gordon. Only one more town before they reached Rushville. They should get there just before dark. About two miles east of Rushville Bill stopped. "This is where we turn south and we want to spend the night on our land", he said. "It'll be dark before we get there, but I'm sure I can find it."

Shaking hands, James said, "Bill, I'll come over and help you get set up first chance I get."

"And I'll come and help you, too, James. We need to work together." James continued on to Rushville. He thought, "I'll spend another night under the wagon rather than sleep in the hotel. That will save money".

The next morning James walked into the Citizens bank and talked to Mr. Musser, "Good morning, I'm James Furman. I'm new in town and I'm on my way to my homestead claim south of town. I plan to be here for the rest of my life. Starting up anew probably means I'll need to borrow some money and I hope you will be willing to loan me as I need it."

"Mr. Furman, do you have anything to secure the loan?"

"Just my good name and I'm a hard worker."

"I'm sure that is true Mr. Furman, but the bank cannot loan money unless you have something of value to use as collateral." James had never thought about needing collateral.

Next James approached the owner of the general store; the outcome was the same. He left town disappointed because no one was willing to give him credit. People were friendly enough, but where money was involved, he would have to prove his honesty and financial ability first. He took encouragement from the knowledge that he would be on his land that day.

After buying some food and seed for a garden, he left town for the 12 miles to the homestead. Once again he stood on the bluff overlooking the river, admiring the view. Making his way down to the bottom, he found a place to set up camp. The first day on his own land was ending.

James was up before sunrise. This would be a day of decisions. Where to plant? Where to put a house? Up on the bluff the land was flat and would be good for crops, but across the river in the cottonwood trees would be better for a home. However, having the crops on one side of the river and a house on the other side didn't seem like a good idea. He crossed the river and rode around in all directions. Finally he picked a place for a house on the side of a hill, which would be out of the wind and not far from the river. There were not enough trees nearby for a cabin, so it would have to be a sod house.

He said to himself, "I hope Belle can accept living in a sod house." Close-by was a level enough place to plant crops. Not as big as James would have liked, but it would do for a start. "I have a plan in mind now. Wonder if Bill has started anything? Think I'll go over and see how he is doing."

The next morning James headed east, then north, in search of the Jansen's. It was not difficult to get lost in the hills but James had always had a good sense of direction. It only took two wide circles to find them. Bill had already started to lay sod blocks for a house. He wanted shelter for his wife since she was expecting a baby. James helped Bill for the next three days on the house. As they worked they talked, "Bill, have you decided where to plant"

"I have a place in mind. My concern is that neither of us has a disk."

"True, but I've noticed that the soil is sandy and loose in a lot of places. Do you think we might work the soil with just a plow by going across the field twice; the second time crosswise?"

"I thought about the same thing, James. Seems to me that is about our only choice."

"One more thing, since you are helping me with a house, it's only right that we do some work on your place when we get finished here. Maybe we can try our plowing idea on your place."

Mary went with them and while the two men broke ground, Mary prepared meals, but mostly rested. Two days later seed was in the ground. The cross plowing did not work well; however, the soil was loose enough that it could be smoothed out by dragging a log across it. After the seed was planted, they drug limbs over the soil to cover the seed. "Bill, it's your turn. There still is enough daylight to get to your place and we could start breaking the ground the first thing in the morning."

The next morning, plowing began on Bill's place and a day and a half later seed had been planted. "Bill, it's a good feeling to have finished; let's pray for good yields this fall."

"It sure is a good feeling, and praying won't hurt any. How about we rest for a day or two?"

"I would like to do that, but I'd better go back and start a house for Belle and me now. Maybe in a few days you could come over to help finish it."

"Give me three or four days and I'll come and help." That evening it rained, which was good for the just planted seeds. But since James had only the wagon for shelter, he stayed under it and ate a cold supper. Tomorrow he would begin on a home.

James soon realized house-building was going to be a problem. The nearby soil was too sandy to form into blocks. The second problem was that there were not enough trees nearby to build a cabin. His only option was to build something like he saw at Jules' home. So he started digging into the hillside and hollowed out a cave-like area. Next he found ground near the river that was moist enough and with enough grass that he could make sod blocks. These he hauled back to the cave in the wagon and laid them perpendicular to the opening in the hillside.

Before these walls were finished, Bill Jansen showed up. With both men working it didn't take long to finish the walls. Bill stayed until some trees were cut down and the trunks split for the roof and put into place. After Bill left, James piled dirt on top of the roof to stop rainwater from falling inside. He also closed in the front with some of the remaining split logs and sod blocks.

As James stood looking at what he had completed, he thought for the second time, "Can Belle accept living in such a place? I must at least get a window put in before she comes." Next he needed to make some kind of place to keep the cow and horses. One day was spent riding up and down the riverbanks searching for big limbs or anything that he could use to make a corral. Using what was left from the trees he and Bill had cut, along with what he was able to find, plus some rope, he patched together a corral. It was time to write to Belle.

He thought a long time about what words to use in describing their new "home." He really did not want to tell her; yet – he could not let her be surprised, or worse, shocked. Finally he tried to be honest but not completely detailed.

Dear Belle,

The land here is a pretty green on rolling hills and there's a nice river close to our new home. Not deep, but they say it always has water in it. The sky is the purest blue that I have ever seen. Wait till you see it. Rushville is a booming town of 400 people and the county seat; that tells you it's of some importance. It also has two general stores, a grocery store, restaurant, hotel, even a millinery store and a shoe shop. There's a newspaper published once a week and they're building a new school. There are even three churches. So it really is a civilized town. And, there aren't many Indians.

Our home is not much right now but it's the best I could do with what was available. It's not a house like you are living in now, but it'll provide good protection from rain and snow. I promise you there will be a true house as soon as possible.

I miss you and Edna so much and want you to come now. Start making plans!

Love, James

He went to town to mail his letter and to buy some food. Now there was not enough money left to buy anything. While he was at the general store he asked, "You know of someplace where a person could find work?"

The storeowner answered, "I think the railroad is hiring men, you might try there." After other inquiries, there seemed to be just one choice, the railroad. The railroad was still expanding north and west. They were laying tracks to Rapid City and the Black Hills. This was not what James had in mind, but he did need money if he was going to buy a window and other necessary things. The man at the rail office informed him the railroad did need workers 30 miles on west. He could ride the train to the end of the line, if he wanted a job.

After a sleepless night James took his animals over to Bill Jansen and asked, "Would you feed and look after my animals while I'm working on the railroad? They are laying new tracks into the Dakota's and I can get work there. I hope to be gone only a month or so."

"Sure I will. I will even take you to the train." James hoped his being gone for a while would not go against him at the claim office. He did not plan to be gone long.

James returned six weeks later with enough money to last awhile and to buy the window. James had not minded the hard work, but the workers' drinking and gambling were not his lifestyle. He was thankful to be back on the homestead. There was one thing missing, his family.

James wanted his family with him. Once again he wrote, hoping, yet fearful of how Belle would accept the condition they must live in. He asked her to bring clothes, dishes, household goods, whatever she felt might be needed, and his violin. He would meet her at the train in Rushville.

Belle read the letter and thought to herself, what was this place going to be like? She realized it would be much more primitive than where they lived in Iowa. She felt James was not telling her everything. Also he only spoke of one neighbor. Could she live like that? After looking at baby Edna, she knew her place was with her husband.

She told herself, "I can adapt." She made the preparations to go. Even though she was fearful of going, she would make the trip. Then the thought of doing this alone frightened her more. "I have never been on a train. Can I manage transferring the baggage from one train to another?" She thought about writing James and telling him to come and get her. Belle wrote back; she would leave in a week, which would be July 10, 1887.

When she announced she was leaving to join her husband, Mary Pearl, her mother-in-law told her, "I am going with you." Belle had not asked for help. She didn't know whether to be glad or fearful. One never knew what Mary Pearl's conduct might be. Belle had always wondered how Mary's husband had lived with her; no surprise that he had left her. The family did not talk about him. James said he went back to Pennsylvania to die. Belle had trouble just being around her for short periods of time. Besides her personality, Belle did not approve of Mary Pearl's smoking a pipe.

Her going would mean being with her for days. Still she thought, "It would be good not to be alone traveling into an area still regarded as the frontier." She felt better after Mary told her, "I just wanted to see for myself what the country looks like. I don't plan to stay. I'll return to Iowa after I see the land." Could it be that Mary Pearl really was concerned about Belle and Edna making the trip alone? Maybe she just didn't know how to say that.

On the train to Webster City and to Sioux City there were normal passenger cars, but from there on Belle was introduced to immigrant cars. These cars did not have seats, just backless benches crossways in the car with a potbelly stove in the middle. Belle was glad it was not wintertime. If one wanted to sleep, a straw-filled mattress could be rented for $1.25 to $2.50, depending on the person's bargaining powers. Then room between benches or in the aisle had to be found. Everyone's baggage was piled in the back of the car. There was no comfort to be had on this car. Fortunately they had been told to take food and water with them before they got on the train. It was a very tiring trip and Edna fussed most of the way. Mary Pearl was no help with Edna, but did see to the transfer of the baggage.

When they reached Rushville, there was James! He had grown a beard and was wearing a broad-brimmed hat. He had a big smile on his face. "Belle, you don't know how much I missed you and Edna. It is so good to see you both." Then James' mouth dropped open when he saw his mother. What a shock! "Mother, I didn't know you were coming, too. You might want to stay in town; we don't have a spare bedroom."

"No, I want to see your homestead." There was nothing to do but for all of them to go to the homestead.

After driving away from the train depot, Belle noticed a group of people standing outside of a building. "Are those people Indians?"

"Yes, they are. The Indian supply depot for the Sioux reservation is here in Rushville. But there've been no problems."

"I feel a little nervous about that. Are you sure there are no problems?"

"Yes, Belle, they are very peaceable. See the tall man leaning against the post? His name is Charlie Whitebelly. He works part of the time for some of the ranchers. They say he is a good worker."

"What a strange name – Whitebelly! Is that really his name?"

"Yes. When an Indian baby is born, whatever the first thing the parents see is the name given to the baby. Charlie is what the white folks added."

On the way James pointed out every positive thing he could think of. "See those milky blue flowers over there? They're called Bluebells. You need to smell them in early June. They have a strong fragrance."

James stopped on top of the bluff, he pointed to the river below and then out to the horizon. He hoped the view would impress his wife as much as it had impressed him. The sun was low and the sky clear. James put his arm around Belle, "Tell me what you see." Her answer was not quite what he had hoped for, but she did seem impressed.

"What is the name of the river?"

"The Niobrara; in the Sioux Lakota language the word means 'running water'. Someone told me it starts up in the Wyoming mountains."

The Bluff on the North side of the River

Niobrara River

They drove down the hill and across the river. Belle's reaction to the "home" was not as bad as James had feared but he could tell she was disappointed. He quickly said,"It won't be forever. We will have a true house as soon as possible." He was glad he had gotten the window installed. Mary Pearl did not make any comment.

James had made a crib-like bed for Edna. And with some of the money he had earned, he had bought a cooking stove. However, having a bed for company had never crossed James' mind. Where to put Mary Pearl was a problem. For once in her life Mary thought of someone other than herself. Sensing the delicate situation of sleeping arrangements, Mary blurted out, "I'll sleep in the wagon tonight. It won't be the first time I done that."

James could not imagine his mother ever sleeping in a wagon; maybe she had when his family left Pennsylvania. He was just glad she had settled the issue, at least for the night. After just one day Mary Pearl was ready to return home. On the way back to town Mary asked, "James, what is it you see in this country, it looks desolate to me."

"Mother, look, you can see to the horizon in every direction. There is nothing to hinder you and that gives me a feeling of freedom I have never felt before." He continued, "Here I have the chance to own more land than I ever dreamed of owning. Here I have the opportunity and satisfaction of building a place where nothing has ever been built before. That thought makes it very special."

Mary listened for awhile, and then asked, "Is there any more unclaimed land?" Would his mother never cease to surprise him!

"Yes, there is. As matter of fact, the quarter section just south of our homestead was unclaimed."

Mary Pearl said, "Then I am going to file on it."

"Mother, do you realize that you would have to live on the claim for five years?"

"I am aware of that. I want you to have it surveyed and mail me the location of the boundaries. I'll do the filing and move onto the claim." James stayed with his mother until the train left, and then he returned to the homestead. All the way back he was worried about Belle. How did she do alone for an afternoon?

While he was gone, the Jansen's had come to meet Belle. So she had not been alone. Belle liked Mary Jansen. A bond quickly developed between Belle and Mary. They were two young women who had followed their husbands who wanted to fulfill their dreams. They would keep in touch and help one another. This made James feel better about bringing his family to the Nebraska prairie. That night James shaved off his beard but he would keep the mustache for the rest of his life.

The days of summer came and went while James and Belle settled into their routines. The joys of married life overcame what daily problems arose. A satisfying marriage bed works wonders. Yet Belle still struggled with the loneliness and crudeness of prairie life. Worst of all were the bites from flies, mosquitoes, and sand fleas. She was a lady of culture and refinement. Now she lived in a dugout with a dirt floor. She had to cope with insects and all kinds of varmints including snakes that would crawl in. This was not going to be the life she envisioned. One time a bird got inside and Belle chased it for 30 minutes while Edna laughed and thought it was great fun.

When it rained James would run up on the roof to throw on more dirt, but the dirt would turn to mud and leaked down through the roof. This necessitated the cleaning and washing of everything inside.

The one thing she would not accept was bathing in the river. She preferred to use a bucket for her bath. Belle made the soap that was used for bathing and washing clothes. She put animal fat, lye and borax in a big cauldron half full of water. This was placed on an outdoor fire. She would stir with a large paddle until it had cooked sufficiently. Then after cooling for two days, it was cut into bars and set aside to cure.

Belle enjoyed the rare trips to Rushville. She liked being around people. She struggled with the loneliness. For days on end there was no one but James and Edna, and James would be away from the house much of the time. So when James went to town or they needed food, Belle would plan on going, too. Visits with the Jansen's from time to time were very special for Belle.

The day arrived when Belle would make her first trip into town by herself. She worried about finding her way back home because she had never been good with directions. She formed a plan. She would take old rags and tear them into strips. These she would tie to weeds and drive until she could barely see the rag, stop, get out of the wagon and tie another rag onto a weed. She continued this all the way to town. The return trip went quicker.

James got the quarter section south of them surveyed for his mother but he doubted she would follow through on her statement. He also spent time hunting prairie chickens, rabbits or a deer so they could have fresh meat.

Belle occupied her time by sewing dresses for Edna and keeping their home as clean as she could. She also took pride in caring for the garden, which would be a main source of food. By necessity she had learned to make candles and to dry meat, as well as making soap.

The weather had been good and the rains plentiful enough for good crops to develop. Plus the garden had yielded more than enough vegetables to last through the winter. Belle canned all summer long and

James dug another cave to store grain for the animals and vegetables for the winter. The problem was keeping varmints out of it.

When it came time to harvest the crops, James contacted the nearby cattlemen and some people in town in hopes of selling some of what he had raised. He could have sold more if he had more. The crop money allowed him to buy a plow and a disc. By the late fall everything looked great for the two homesteaders.

James even considered buying the quarter section on their northern boundary. This he could do through the Homestead Act for $1.25 per acre. The quarter section north of the river was available. In James' mind the more land he owned, the more money he could earn. James thought it was a good idea; Belle was not so sure. "James, you told me we would have a real house. I don't enjoy the bugs and spiders, let alone the snakes in this place where we have to live! Nor do I like Edna crawling around on a dirt floor. Now you want to buy more land? We need a real house." She also had something else to think about. She was expecting their second child.

"You're right. This isn't the time to be thinking about buying more land, besides we have plenty to do getting ready for winter. I still hope to buy more land, but maybe that quarter section will still be there later."

Everything seemed to have fallen into place for James and Belle. The weather had been good and the harvest successful and they had friends and some new neighbors, even though they were miles apart. Edna had done well and was healthy.

On a bright fall morning James said, "The geese are starting south again. I saw some on the river yesterday. I'll shoot two or three this evening. It'll give us something different to eat."

With winter coming they were not certain what to expect. They knew there would be snow and cold, but how much? The people in town had told them that storms could come upon them quickly and that deep snows would prevent travel for days sometimes. If James had been right on where to put the dugout, the snow should not drift too badly in front of their door. The animals would have some shelter from the cottonwood trees and the hill to the north. And they were within 150 yards of the dugout. The second dugout with the grain and canned food was between the house dugout and the corral.

They would just have to wait and see, but they felt they could handle what came. Thirty days later they found themselves in one of the worst blizzards to ever hit the prairie.

CHAPTER 3
A TIME TO BE BORN

The morning of November 22, 1887 began fair and warm. James had left to hunt prairie chickens and Belle was bathing Edna and thinking about preparing food for lunch. Without warning the temperature dropped 60 degrees in two hours. Ominous clouds filled the sky and the snow began. (A few years later this winter would be referred to as the winter of "Blue Snow".) The snow fell at an increasing rate. The wind was blowing so strong that James had to lean forward to walk into it. James thought, "I had better go back to the dugout." Halfway back he could barely see where he was going. The snow was not falling; it was going sideways and getting deeper.

Fortunately before the snow became deep, Belle brought into the dugout a supply of wood and corncobs for the stove. As snow and wind increased in intensity, she became concerned, and then she grew frightened. "Where is James? Is he lost? I can't see anything but white through the window." It was impossible to see two inches away from the window because of the heavy and fast snowfall. She thought to herself, "I must remain calm."

James was certain he was going in the right direction but he was not sure how close he was to the dugout. He asked himself, "How far had I gone before the snow started? It seems like I have walked five miles at least, but I can't possibly have gone that far." He became concerned and he was cold; he had not put on a heavy coat when he left. He told himself, "Stay calm. It can't be much farther." Finally he either hit or fell into the rope section of the corral. The shotgun fell someplace in the snow. That was not important now. "This has got to be the corral rope! I have got to be close. I'll move left if I'm where I think I am, then the dugout should be back about 150 yards." Holding onto the rope with numb hands, he worked his way left and then turned toward what he hoped would take him to the dugout door.

He counted his steps; when he reached 100, he yelled "Belle". There was no answer, just the sound of the howling wind. The snow was over his knees. Exhaustion was overtaking James. He thought, "Am I going to die this close to the dugout door?" He went another 50 steps and fell over something. It was a chair Belle had left in front of the dugout. Getting up he looked around; he had to be right in front of the dugout and within 10 feet of it. But he could not see it because of the falling snow. He yelled again, "Belle", but no answer.

He left the chair directly behind him, and then walked forward, with his hands held out. He walked into the front of the dugout. "Thank you, Lord!" was the only thought in James' mind. He felt his way to the door and pulled with what strength he had left. The snow in front of the door made it difficult to open. When Belle realized what was going on, she pushed on the door from the inside. Finally it opened enough for James to slide through and fall to the floor. Belle pulled the door closed again.

James lay shivering on the dirt floor while Belle cried. As she helped him to a chair and covered him with blankets and coats, she said, "Oh, James, I was so afraid you were out there someplace frozen. I'll bring you some hot coffee. That will help warm you up." James just shook. He was grateful to be out of the wind and snow.

The blizzard continued the rest of the day, throughout the night and into the next day. Around four o'clock in the afternoon it stopped. The window was covered with so much ice and snow; only a dim light could be seen through it. The wind no longer howled. James tried the door. It would not open. He pushed again, harder this time and the door moved slightly. Using the iron rod they used as a fire poker, he pushed on the door and wedged the iron rod between the door and the doorframe. Then he pushed and moved the iron rod back and forth until the door opened enough to see out.

The snow was over four feet deep in front of the door. Using all his strength, he pushed again and got it open enough to squeeze outside. "Belle, find something I can use to scoop snow away from the door." She handed him a pie pan. With the pie pan he moved snow away from the door freeing it to open and close. He now realized the front of the dugout should have faced some other direction.

His next thought was of the animals. Wading through snow almost to his waist, he finally made it to the cottonwood grove. There he found the two horses and they were standing side-by-side, facing opposite directions. But James could not see the cow! Struggling through the snow he circled around for an hour. He could not find the cow. He returned to the dugout, thinking I'll search farther tomorrow. The next day the snow fell again and the wind blew. It was another blizzard.

For the next six weeks, at least once a week there was a blizzard. Surviving became the daily task. Something to burn for heat was the first priority. Something to eat was number two. They melted snow for water every day. They were fortunate in that they had only been without anything to burn in the stove for one day. What wood they had in the house was exhausted, the cow chips were gone, and even the corncobs had given out.

The two horses were struggling, too. They had gotten to the second dugout which gave them some protection and food until all the grain was gone. In the process they had broken most of the glass jars of food Belle had prepared. James never found the cow until the snow melted. Then he also found the shotgun he had dropped. Human endurance had been tested and they had survived.

When the snow finally stopped falling and the sun came out, Belle asked, "How do you think others have survived the blizzards?"

"I don't know. Maybe when it melts a little more we should try to go to the Sweeney place. It is too far to the Jansen place in all this snow." Harold and Heidi Sweeney were a young couple that had come from Wisconsin. They had only homesteaded for a few months before the first blizzard.

They bundled up Edna, got in the wagon and started out. James tried to stay on high ground where the snow had blown away and there were no drifts. It was difficult but they made it to Sweeney's sod house. "Hello, anybody here?" There was no answer.

The door was closed and there was not a lot of snow in front of it. James and Belle knocked on the door.

There was no answer, so they pulled the door open. Inside there was no fire. It was cold. Heidi was sitting in a chair in hysterics. She was not capable of normal conversation. Harold was not inside. James went out to look for him while Belle tried to calm Heidi. "It will be alright, Heidi. I'll start a fire and make some coffee. Did Harold go for help?" The answer was one word, "Harold?"

James came back inside 30 minutes later, "I can't find Harold. There are no footprints anyplace." When the snow was completely melted, Harold's body was found in a low place 70 yards away from the house. He had apparently been out when the first blizzard hit and had not made it back to the house. James and Belle took Heidi home with them. It was several days before Heidi's condition improved.

When spring of 1888 began and James and Belle could make it to Rushville, they took Heidi to the train station and put her on a train to Wisconsin. While they were in town, they discovered 30 people had died and there was a loss of more than 3,000 head of cattle. No one was untouched. Burying people and disposing of dead cattle would have to wait until the snow was gone and the ground was not frozen.

Even the train had not traveled through town for 30 days. The storekeepers raised prices on what was available. But at the same time they were willing to extend credit rather freely. People in town and all around were trying to cope with the conditions. Everyone came together to help one another. All the churches had special services to give thanks for the end of winter and mourn those who had died.

Finally the weather became warmer. Summer came and Mother Nature allowed another calamity. It was very hot and dry. The temperature was over 100 degrees many days and no rain fell all summer. The only good thing was there were fewer mosquitoes. The newly planted crops were burning up and would not produce. The Niobrara River was nothing but a small stream. The money James and Belle had made from the first year's crop was gone.

Belle was due to deliver their second child and she wanted to go back to Iowa. "Belle, things do look bad but I don't want to give up so soon. Let's stay awhile longer. If something doesn't work out then, I'll agree to go back to Iowa."

Then a letter came; Mary Pearl had filed a claim on the land next to them and was on her way there. She had sold her Iowa farm to James' brothers and she wanted James or someone to build her a house. They could not believe what they read. James had written his mother that conditions had changed for the worse and they were even thinking of going back to Iowa. Belle was even more upset because she and her mother-in-law had never been compatible. There had been times when Mary Pearl would not even speak to Belle. Now she was going to be a neighbor.

"James, you know how your mother treats me. Stop her from coming!"

"She's my mother; how can I tell her not to move out here?"

"Please, James, try to talk her out of living here."

"Alright. I'll try."

When Mary Pearl arrived, James met her. "Mother, conditions here are terrible! The best thing you can do is to go back to Iowa."

"Nonsense! Do you think one bad winter and one bad summer are going to forever ruin things?" She would stay, in town that is, until she had a house. "I have enough cash from the sale of the farm to build a house and then some. I want you to find someone to build a house, not a sod one." So James bought wood and enlisted help from Bill Jensen to build her a house, which provided James and Belle with a little money again.

While the house was being constructed, Belle went into labor. James ran for help to the closest neighbor, the Preston's, who had taken over the Sweeney property. "Mrs. Preston, we need help. Belle is about to deliver!" Mrs. Preston was willing but she had scant knowledge of what to do if things did not go well. The baby was unduly large and for a time it looked very serious for mother and baby. Help came from an unexpected source. Without warning, in walked Mary Pearl, who had learned of the coming birth from Mr. Preston. She promptly took over. She had worked for a doctor back east and was able to deliver the baby. Both Belle and the baby would live. Mary Pearl returned to town as soon as the baby was cleaned up. The baby boy was named Evan.

It would seem that such an intimate experience between the two women would have softened their relationship, but it did not. Mary Pearl would now be their closest neighbor and there would be considerable contact between them. Compatibility with her would be difficult for Belle. James would farm her land as well as their own. She was also the children's grandmother and could not be denied that relationship.

The second year had been very hard. Money had been so scarce that much consideration was given to buying a two-cent stamp to mail a letter. By necessity Belle quickly learned to scrimp and save. She made their clothes from feed sacks from the mill where James had worked from time to time. When the flies and bugs, and her relationship with her mother-in-law, became more than she could endure, Belle would retreat to a grove of pine trees. In solitude she would weep and listen to the soothing whisper of the pines. After being comforted by nature, she would regain her composure and go back to face the problems of the day.

James had been frustrated watching the crops dry up and not being able to do anything about it. There would be no money from a harvest. The money he earned from building his mother's house might not see them through the next winter and buy seed in the spring. He was able to work some at the mill, which provided additional funds. What about next year or the year after that? Could he provide for his family by farming? His concern led him to the decision to raise cattle as well as farm. He discussed this with Belle.

"James, I think we should go back to Iowa. It's better there. We may not even get any vegetables from the garden this year. I've been carrying buckets and buckets of water from the river to water some of the plants, but I can't water the entire garden. You said if things didn't work out we would go back. Well, they're not getting any better."

"Belle, we don't know if it is any better in Iowa and we just can't give up and lose this land. It's not always going to be this bad. We can make it. Right now we need something good – something special. How about some of your cinnamon rolls? They would taste great right now."

"Just like a man! Things are bad and you just think about food."

"I'm just trying to think of something pleasant and nice."

"I'm not sure I should make any cinnamon rolls. There's not much flour and there is only two cups of sugar left. I don't know how long that will have to last." Belle was not so sure they should stay but felt she must support her husband.

Soon fortune began to smile on them. The weather turned cooler and rains came again. The garden would provide food, and the grass and the crops began growing. More importantly, there was a family that was going back east and they had 10 beef cows they wanted to sell. They were priced for a quick sale. James and Belle bought the cows. The ability to raise cattle would begin.

Now there was no money to buy seed in the spring for another crop. James must again find work someplace to supplement their finances. The food and anything else they needed would have to come from some other source. This was a big risk. James worked anyplace he could find work that next year, mostly at the mill. His reputation as an honest hard-working man grew. Mary Pearl thought James' idea to raise cattle was a good idea, so she bought 15 cows and a bull.

When Evan was a year old, Mary Pearl became very sick and had to live with James and Belle for awhile. When she moved in she brought with her a pet ferret that was great for keeping mice away but was not a typical house pet. One day as Evan lay napping, the ferret bit a chunk out of Evan's left ear. That was it. Belle could take no more. Both sides said harsh words. Mary Pearl moved back to her own house.

Slowly but surely finances improved. During the years of blizzards, the sand hills were not quite as severely hit as the rest of the country where entire herds of cattle had been wiped out. The revival of the cattle business would begin in the sand hills. This revival introduced Herefords and Angus cattle, which were superior to the longhorn. The railroad expanded the cattle market to the east. No longer was the Indian agent the only cattle buyer. Cattle raising had a bright future.

A year later in 1890, James and Belle were able to pay $1.25 per acre for an adjoining quarter section of land. They also had increased their "herd" to 35 cows and a bull. The new animals were Black Angus. James was proud of the Angus cattle. They fared well on prairie grass and they withstood the Nebraska winters well.

James started thinking he had better begin branding their cattle. He wasn't sure just what kind of mark to use. "Belle, we need to brand our cattle so we can prove they belong to us. Do you have any suggestions for a brand mark?"

After thinking for a few minutes, Belle said, "I remember when I first saw this place from the top of the bluff. I thought as I looked out how the grass blowing in the wind looked like the waves of an ocean. You went across this ocean of grass and threw out an anchor at this spot. And we have been anchored here ever since. So maybe the brand should be an anchor."

"That's a good idea. And maybe we could use the letter F as the shaft." He had not registered his brand but felt the next time he was in town he should do so. He was relieved to find no one had registered a brand like his when he went to the county clerk's office.

Sheridan County records

Brand record

While James was in the clerk's office, Belle picked up their mail and went to the store for groceries. On the way home she handed James a letter from his brothers. After reading it he had a surprised look on his face. "Willie wants to try his hand at homesteading. He wants to know if I will help him find some land and get established."

"That sounds like a fine thing."

"I'm not so sure. Willie was never much of a worker."

"Oh, James, he may have changed. After all, he is your brother. And he could help your mother."

"I know. I'll write to him."

Two months later Willie arrived in Rushville and moved in with James and Belle.

The purchase of additional land and more cows meant they had to borrow from the bank. It also meant James needed to work in town. James worked many days at the mill in Rushville. On the days he worked, it would be well after dark when he reached home. His reputation for hard work and honesty was a deciding point in obtaining the loan. Besides trying to establish a herd of cattle, he still planted wheat and some corn. The corn never did very well, but it was good for supplemental feed for the cows. Including his mother's land, James could use 480 acres for pasture and farming, and still have available unclaimed land to cut wild grass for hay.

Their children now numbered three with the birth of Ava Pearl in 1889. They had moved out of the dugout and built a small three-room house in the cottonwood grove. James also dug a well for water. Belle felt normal again. There were now wood floors! The walls of the house were upright boards with an outside siding. The space between was filled with dirt. This provided good insulation until the inside boards began to crack open and the dirt fell out onto the room. Belle lined the inside walls with unbleached muslin, which helped stop any dirt from sifting out. The ability to do such a thing was evident of their emerging from the crushing poverty of their second year; because muslin cost five cents per yard! There was a barn and a milk cow; there were chickens and a chicken house, and a fence around the house.

Mary Pearl was still a pain in the neck for Belle. Their relationship never improved. Mary Pearl was a cantankerous woman that Belle could never please. But at least Belle did not have to face the crudeness of the dugout anymore. James would be out working during the day on their land. He no longer had to work for others. Belle would care for the children and the house.

On Sundays the work would be only what was necessary. On many a Sunday afternoon James would play his violin and Belle would read to the children. Once again life seemed good to James and Belle. James began to think about filing for another quarter section of land while Belle was thinking about Edna needing schooling and it was 12 miles to town. There would still be bad winters and hot dry summers to face, but they were better prepared for them now.

Early one June day a storm came. There was not much rain but a lot of thunder and lightning. A bolt of lightning hit the dry grass north of the river. James had been working in the barn and as he headed toward the house, he saw smoke in the north. The cattle were there! As he saddled a horse, he yelled, "Belle…Belle, go for help!" Then he rode across the river toward the smoke. When he reached the top of the bluff he saw a five foot red/orange wall of fire whipped around by the wind. It started west of the fence and extended one half mile eastward. Calves were bawling and cows were going in all directions.

James forced the reluctant horse forward until he was between the cattle and the flames. He worked the horse back and forth between the fire and the cattle, trying to move them away and toward the river.

Belle hitched a horse to the buggy and loaded the kids into it and started across the river. By the time she got to the top of the bluff it was too late to go anyplace but back south. She could see James driving the cattle toward the river. She pulled over on the east side of the trail in an effort to create a chute for the cattle to follow the road down to the river. She got out of the buggy and stood in front of the horse, holding tightly to the reins. "Edna and Evan, stand up and wave your arms when the cattle get to us."

James was having a difficult time trying to keep the cattle together and moving toward the river. Occasionally a maverick would break off and run back. James would make an attempt to get it back in the group but if he was not successful on the first attempt, he would have to let it go and hope it would follow. The fire was moving fast toward them and seemed to cover the entire horizon.

As the cattle approached where Belle was standing, they stopped. The children were waving their arms too early. The cattle were bellowing loudly and turning in all directions. Belle told the kids not to move and James gently moved them forward again. First one then another began going down the trail to the river. Soon the rest followed down into the water. They stopped in the middle of the river. James and Belle looked back to see two cows running around in a crazed manner. There was nothing they could do.

They, too, descended to the river, grateful that most of the cattle were safe. The fire stopped at the top of the bluff. There was no more grass for the fire to burn. Some sparks flew off the bluff but fell harmlessly into the river. James, on his horse, and Belle, in the buggy with the kids, remained in the river for another 30 minutes or so. They watched the fire die. Fortunately the wind direction prevented the fire from spreading to the east. Both realized what might have been and they were grateful that only two cows were lost. A total disaster had been avoided. Still unless there were good rainfalls in the next six or seven weeks, a quarter section would not have grass until next spring.

Chapter 4

A Time to Be Silent and a Time to Speak

After the fire, there was plentiful rainfall and the crop harvest was very good and the grass made more than enough hay for the next winter. James and Belle had a decent income that year from the sale of wheat and cattle. Life was good for the Furman family, but a sad year for the Sioux Indians who lived 10 miles or so north of Rushville on the Pine Ridge Reservation. Belle no longer felt threatened by Indian trouble.

Their treatment by the government and white settlers had totally demoralized the Indians. One of the reasons for this was the passage of Dawes Act three years earlier. This act intended to divide up reservation land so each male family head would receive 160 acres. This may sound good to a white person but it was not good in the Indian culture. The Dawes Act also intended to move the Indians away from tribal life into a more "civilized" economy and culture.

The cultural change and treatment were more than they could accept. In defense, they turned to spiritualism in the form of the Ghost Dance. They believed dancing the Ghost Dance would bring the Great Spirit to banish the white man from Indian lands and make Indians invulnerable to bullets. Then they could live and hunt as their grand-parents had.

White people became alarmed and frightened over what they saw. Stories began to circulate and grow in the nearby towns. Belle returned from Rushville one day very upset. "James, the Indians are getting ready to attack us! I heard all about it in town today. You need to buy at least two more rifles so we can protect ourselves!"

"Now Belle, calm down. The Indians are not going to attack us. Yes, there is something going on with the Indians that I don't under-stand, but they realize it would be foolish to start anything. Besides, the Indian agent ordered them to stop these demonstrations and the Seventh Cavalry is coming in to back him up."

A week after the Calvary arrived, a gun battle developed on the reservation and Chief Sitting Bull was killed, along with 200 Sioux women and children. What happened at Wounded Knee that day marked another dark episode in Indian-white relationships. It was also the main topic of conversation around Rushville for a long time. Both Indian and white eyewitnesses would relate accounts of what hap-pened, which many times were in disagreement. This time Belle com-mented to James, "How horrible! All those women and children killed; it shouldn't have happened. We should do something to help them."

"Things are pretty touchy up there right now and I don't know what we could do. Better we just stay away."

It was shortly after this Indian scare that neighbor Susan Winston was visiting Belle one afternoon. She stayed longer than she intend-ed and when she realized it was almost dark, the fear of going home overcame her. "Susan, would you like for James and me to take you home?"

"No, just let me borrow an oil lantern. I'll be safe in the light from it." Belle and James held their laughter until she had gone.

In 1891 drought set in; it would be a hard year. For the next 10 years there would only be two years of good rainfall. This was the year that the fourth child, Jay Benjamin was born. For the first part of his life he would be simply known as J.B. Edna was 6 and Belle thought it was time for her to start school. To go 12 miles into town everyday was impossible. "James, we need to build a schoolhouse."

"Do what?"

"Yes, James, Edna needs a proper place to be educated and we can't go to town everyday. Evan, Ava and J.B. will be able to use it. Besides, the neighbor children need a proper place to learn, too."

"A schoolhouse would cost money and I don't have the time to build one. You can teach them in our house."

"No, James, a proper building is needed and I am sure the neighbors will help build it." After a week of this talk, James had heard enough. He talked to two neighbor men and found out Belle had already talked to their wives. The wives had talked to their husbands. A one-room schoolhouse started going up on the land set aside by the government. That fall school began in the new school house.

The school term only lasted three months and Belle was the teacher the first year. She would take J.B. and Ava to school with her, which was not a normal thing to do. But nothing was "normal" in the sand hills in 1890's. People did the best they could with what they had. Sometimes Evan would go too, but he preferred to stay with James. The school was just north of the river. Edna sometimes walked to school. Occasionally she rode a horse the same as the other children. She never wanted to go with her mother; she didn't want other children to know her mother was the teacher.

Rushville had grown. Since it was the official county seat of Sheridan County, even though there was no official court house, people were drawn there for business and transportation needs. There were not only more people, there were more merchants and stores. A new high school had been built in town and there were five churches. When high school was in session the children from the farms and ranches would find someone in town to stay with until the session ended. There were large cattle pens next to the railroad where cattle were loaded to be shipped to Chicago or Omaha. Grain bins and the mill were located there, too, so wheat could be stored and loaded for shipment back east. Progress was the word of the day.

Yet there were problems that last decade of the 19th century. Sometime after the incident at Wounded Knee, the Sioux on the reservation had felt they had been cheated on their food allotment and had been ill-treated when they came into town. They threatened to cause trouble, which stirred up the white folks. Some people became frightened. This problem was short-lived after three young Sioux males were arrested for causing a fight, but in 1892 there was bigger problem spilling over from Wyoming.

The Wyoming Stock Growers Association members, who were owners of large herds, felt that the number of new settlers and soddies that developed in western Nebraska and Wyoming were edging into the open grasslands too much. This area had always been considered free range land where cattle grazed freely. Finally opinions grew so strong that an outright war in Johnson County, Wyoming developed. The U.S. Army was sent in to stop the killings and restore peace.

Some of the gunmen hired by the Wyoming cattlemen went to Chadron to hide out. At the same time in western Nebraska some of the big ranchers began to hire bodyguards and some questionable "cowhands". One was Dave Tate, a Texas gunman. He did not do anymore cow work than a five-year-old. He liked to hang around Gordon and Rushville. He would shoot every cat that crossed his path, even some lying in store windows. The farmers and some small ranchers began to get warnings to get out of the country. Some of the warnings were by letter and some by cowhands riding rough-shod over a small outfit's land.

Two such cowboys went across James' land as he was repairing a fence north of the river. They stopped, "Furman, there has been a lot of trouble around here. It would be best if you took your family and left the country." When James looked up at the men, he happened to see a coyote sitting some 150 yards away. He calmly picked up his rifle from the wagon and killed the coyote. James then turned to the two and said, "I would like to be neighborly with everyone but I expect everyone to be neighborly to me." The two rode off. James and Belle were not threatened again. Others were not so fortunate. West of Rushville one of the farmers who had been warned was found shot. Tate was arrested for the murder but released for lack of evidence.

Old Jules was on his way to Rushville one day and stopped at the Green's place right after they received a warning. Jules read the warning and asked to borrow a horse from them. He rode the horse to the ranch where Tate and some of the others hung out. He had always been treated well there, for everyone knew of Jules' reputation. But on this day they did note the Green's brand on the horse that Jules rode. Jules spent the day there, talking about hunting wolves and he did some long distance target practice while the cowboys were around to watch. It was obvious that he was sending a message. After that there was no more trouble from the large cattlemen around Rushville, but trouble did continue east in Cherry County.

In 1893 James went to Chadron, which was now the closest land office, to sign papers to make his homestead officially his and Belle's. Belle met him at the Rushville train station when he returned. He said to her, "You're not going to believe the news from Chadron. There is going to be a horse race beginning in Chadron and going all the way to Chicago."

"That's ridiculous. Who would ever do anything so foolish?"

"Well, there are nine men signed up for it already. There may be more before it starts next week. It's supposed to go through Rushville. Wouldn't mind going to town to see it."

"Just what do you think you are going to see? And you will never know who wins, so why bother?"

"This will be history in the making and I want to say I saw it. And as for who wins it, the newspapers will report that." James and Evan did go to see the riders go through Rushville. They all were using two horses. People cheered as they rode by.

Two weeks later there was a story in the Rushville Journal about Joe Gillespie being declared the winner of the Chadron to Chicago Cowboy Race. John Berry actually got there first, riding Sandy and Poison. But he was disqualified for having prior knowledge of the race route. Seven of the nine riders finished the race, which ended at Buffalo Bill's Wild West Show.

Evan started to school in the fall of 1893 and the fifth child, Leo, was born.

Willie had now lived with James and Belle off and on for three years. Sometimes he would stay with Mary Pearl. He had never finished the house on his claim, so he spent very little time there. Nor did he do much to help with the work on James and Belle's place. He spent a lot of time in town or stayed around their house. Belle had made some comments to him from time to time about finishing his house and working on his place, but he didn't seem to listen.

One night after supper he took Belle some clothes to wash and said, "I need these socks darned." Belle was nursing Leo and she looked at Willie. With her face turning red, she sternly said, "You do it yourself. I am tired of cooking and washing and doing everything else for you while you do nothing. You don't even help James with all he has to do. You don't even do anything for yourself. I want you out of here."

James took an opened-mouth Willie out onto the porch. "She's right, Willie. The Bible says if you don't work, you don't eat. And you haven't been pulling your own weight. In the morning take your things and move onto your claim. I'll go over with you and help put a roof over what you have started."

"James, you have a wife and children to build something for. I don't have a wife and no prospects to find one. Do you know how lonely it gets by yourself?"

"Willie, rather than feeling sorry for yourself, think about the three years you have spent to get ownership of some land. What do you want to do? If you walk away now you will have nothing. If a life here is not what you want, consider staying on your claim two more years and Belle and I will find some way to buy it from you. Then you'll have a stake to move somewhere else."

"I don't know if I can take the loneliness."

"Go stay with Mother when you get lonely and occasionally come by here for a meal. Belle will still want to see you once in awhile."

"You'll help me finish the house?"

"Yes."

"OK. I'll try to stick it out." Willie did stay the additional two years then sold his homestead to James and Belle.

This was also the year that the bank owner asked James if he would be interested in buying the section north and west of his place. The troubles of the previous year had frightened the land-owner into leaving and since there was a mortgage on the land, the bank needed someone to pay off the loan. Very little had been paid on the loan and the bank would like to collect the balance. James had paid back a previous loan and the bank thought he would repay this loan.

"Belle, we have a great opportunity to own more land. The section northwest of us has been vacated and the bank is offering it to us. This would mean we would own an entire section and we could increase the herd by 50 or more cows."

"James, we need a bigger house, not more land. We have two girls and three boys; we need bedrooms." Being the tightfisted money-saver that she was, Belle had been saving money towards building a new house. "I have been thinking about this for awhile and have even saved some money for a new house. I'm not going to give it up for more land or cattle!"

"Belle, don't you see what this will mean later on?" They talked for a whole week before Belle agreed, and then only if James would promise a new house within two years and to put the title for the new land in her name. With Belle's saved money, James paid part of the cost of the land and bought some more cows and a bull.

Shortly after the papers were signed with the bank, the bank became embroiled in the financial problems of the nation. Panic spread across the country and the effects would be felt until 1900. The Rushville bank did not fail as many other banks across the country did, but it was very close to going under.

The problem occurred when the federal gold reserve began to shrink. When people found out about it, they exchanged their greenback paper dollars for gold because they thought the government was going broke. Then a political fight developed over the backing of federal funds by silver rather than gold. Financial disasters continued until newly mined gold from Alaska restored the gold reserves.

It was during this fear the bank wanted the money for the mortgaged land. "Mr. Furman, we would like for you to pay your loan in full."

James reminded the banker, "You came to me to take the land off the bank's hands. You would have had nothing if we had not accepted your proposition. You'll get your money as soon as we can pay."

When James returned home from town that night, he was still angry. "Belle, the banker was almost demanding me to pay off the loan right then and there! I had to control myself to keep from hitting him in the nose." This would be a time of crushing poverty, but James and Belle weathered the economic conditions through hard work and sacrifice.

A month later James and Evan returned from town and Evan ran into the house yelling, "Buffalo Bill is coming to Rushville! Can we go see his show?" This was big news. People were excited to have a famous person in town. He had renamed his traveling show; it was now "Buffalo Bill's Wild West and Congress of Rough Riders". Rushville was the closest town to the Pine Ridge Indian Reservation and Buffalo Bill needed some Indians for his show. It would be the second time he had shown up. He had lost some of those Indians who had performed for him in the past and he had good luck in hiring the Sioux to perform in his show.

There may have been another reason that Bill liked to work out of Rushville. He handed out scrip to Indians willing to sign up for his show. The scrip was only redeemable at Farmer's Mercantile Co. store in Rushville, owned by Jim Asay. While Mr. Asay was kept busy in the store, Bill would take the owner's wife on a picnic down on the Niobrara River. After he left town there were some reports of Mrs. Asay and Buffalo Bill playing in the river. If James ever saw them, he never said anything.

PICTURE OF BUFFALO BILL'S WILD WEST SHOW ENTOURAGE, TAKEN IN FRONT OF THE ASAY STORE
APRIL 21, 1893. JIM AND MAY ASAY WERE GREAT FRIENDS OF Wm. CODY. 1. JIM ASAY, 2. MAY
ASAY, 4. CHIEF AMERICAN HORSE. 8. THE FAMOUS CHIEF, RED CLOUD.
Ed. GARVEY COLLECTION, COURTESY GFAE LEAHY.

Sheridan County Historical Museum

One of the big social events of the time was a horse race. That would be a day when no work was done. People would come from miles to watch the races and learn all the new gossip. One such race was at White Clay, which was north of Rushville near the reservation. It had been well publicized. It was to be a two horse race between Jim Dahlman on Fiddler and a gray ridden by Tom Brady.

"Belle, children, tomorrow there will be no work. We are going to White Clay to see a horse race."

"Yea", cried the children."

"James, it will take a long day to get there. We would be gone for three days."

"I know that. Don't you think it would be good for all of us to do something different?

"I'll admit I would like to go but what about milking the cow and feeding the chickens?"

"We'll let the cow go one day and the chickens will be alright."

The day before the race James milked early and Edna and Evan fed the chickens. Belle prepared food to take and they left before sun-up in the wagon because the buggy was not big enough to take everything. James drove five or six miles north of Rushville before they stopped to eat. After eating they continued on to White Clay. There were already several wagons and buggies there. James found a place to put the wagon that was not far from where the race would take place. He stretched a tarpaulin out from one side of the wagon and fastened a short pole to each end. Belle prepared a meal over a camp fire. The children were excited about all the people there and the thought of sleeping on the ground.

The next morning more people arrived. Edna asked her mother, "How many people do you think are here?"

"I would say more than 500."

"There are more people here than live in Rushville," Evan said.

Late that morning several men raced their horses trying to prove who was the fastest. The race that everyone came to see was to start at two o'clock. Belle found wives she knew and was thoroughly enjoying herself while the children ran and played. James joined a group of men to discuss cattle and horses, especially which horse was the fastest.

It was a fun-filled day and the gray won. (So did James, but Belle would never know it.) On the way home all the children fell asleep. It was after midnight when they stopped in front of the barn. Belle carried the children into the house while James did the milking by light from a lantern. It had been a long day.

Before the 20th century arrived, there were more changes in the Furman family. Two more daughters were born, Leona and Mary. James was able to keep his word to Belle about building a new house. A two story house was built. It had four bedrooms, a kitchen, and a living room. The money to buy the house came from the sales of good hay yields, and the annual sale of calves, which was now possible. The children were excited about moving. But their enthusiasm plummeted when they found out they would still have to feed the chickens and hogs, carry wood and water into the house, hoe the garden and continue doing all their other chores.

Belle was pleased with the larger house. She even had a new piano, which she had missed being able to play. Music could be heard coming from the house on a warm summer evening. Belle would play the piano and James would play the violin. The children were becoming music lovers.

Edna was developing into a proper young lady, except for one occasion when she tested her mother's temper. Edna had a dress that she did not like, so one day when her father was leaving for town, she sat down on the ground and held on to the back of the buggy while James drove off. She held on until her dress was totally ruined. As punishment Edna would do extra chores for the next month.

Evan was a mischievous boy. He was a jokester, which got him into trouble more than once. Like one cold morning at school, he and another boy peed in a can and set it on top of the potbelly stove. Soon the smell alerted the teacher of the problem. Evan and the other boy ran out the door with the teacher not far behind. The two boys made it up a tree before the teacher reached them. They thought it best to remain there the rest of the day. Evan felt his father's razor strop that night.

The man who taught school to the Furman children, and the other children who lived close enough to ride a horse to the school, lived in the old house. When school was not in session the man would work for James in exchange for free rent. He was not a strong man, but he was helpful. He taught James how to keep records on crop yields and cattle breeding.

Also they added another half section of land to their ranch and bought more cattle. A loan from the bank provided the money. James now spent more time raising cattle and less time farming. Still he continued to plant some corn and wheat. By the end of the 1890's Evan was old enough to be of some help with animals and do some chores. But he was limited by his small size.

In 1893 Mary Pearl made the trip to Chadron with proof of fulfilling her homestead claim. Later in 1895 she filed a timber claim. The required trees were planted but they never grew to any size. She did fulfill all the requirements for ownership and in due time received title to the land.

The unclaimed land was beginning to shrink by the year 1900. Land ownerships changed because of people growing tired of the struggles to survive. The blizzards in winter, the hot dry summers, and the threats on their lives were too much for some. They just gave up and left. Those that did stay bought the land of those that left, or they might refile a new homestead claim for the deserted land.

Leo,   James,   Evan,   Edna,   J. B.,   Belle

Ava

L to R   Furman family   cir. 1896

Back Row L to R: J. B. Furman, Edna Furman, Ava Furman, Mary Furman, Evan Furman.
Front Row L to R: Leona Furman, J. L. Furman, Belle Wicks (Furman), Leo Furman.

Cir.1918

CHAPTER 5
A TIME TO BUILD

The 20th century began with new hope and optimism. James and Belle were out of debt and they anticipated making $500 this year. James was thinking about buying more land again when a different opportunity presented itself. The mill owner died and his widow, Mildred Green, asked James if he would come and see her. "James, you have worked for my husband several times and you have become one of our friends. I don't know how to run the mill and I'm not sure I even want to. Would you be interested in buying the mill? You already know all about operating it."

"Ma'am, true I know the operation and since it is the only mill for miles around, it would be a good thing to own. But there is a problem: money. We just paid off all our debts, and I don't want to mortgage everything again."

"Well, think about it. I'll work with you on the money part as long as I wind up with money to live out my life."

That night he talked to Belle. "What would you think about buying the mill? Mrs. Green asked me if I would be interested in buying it. Said she didn't know how or want to operate it."

"James, I'm surprised; all you have ever talked about was farming and raising cattle."

"True, but this seems like a good move. The mill does a good business; it would provide an additional source of income."

"James, how are you going to take care of this place and spend time in town running the mill? You would work yourself to death. Even if you could do both, I don't want to go back into debt and have to struggle to live."

"Belle, I can do both; it will just take a little adjusting." (James always felt things were possible.) "Besides, Evan is 13 years old now. He can do a lot more of the work around here."

"I can't believe you just said that. Think about how we have been concerned that Evan might be a midget. He is just not big enough to do a man's work. He's too small and you know it!" (Evan did not seem to grow until he was 16, then he shot up overnight to a height of six feet.) "Why, the other day I sent Evan to town to buy some things and as he drove out I couldn't see his head over the buggy seat back."

"I agree with you there. Guess I wasn't thinking clearly. What if I could find a partner? That would mean less money on our part and it would split the time at the mill." Belle began to soften. But who could be the partner?

"You find a partner, then let's talk about it some more."

James went to the bank later that week. "Mrs. Green wants to sell the mill to me, but I don't have the cash and I don't want to mortgage our land again. So if I did try to buy the mill, I would have to borrow some money and I would need a partner. Do you know anyone that might be interested and would be a good partner?"

The banker suggested David Nutt, the blacksmith, might be interested. "I was talking to the blacksmith a few days ago and he said he was interested in expanding into some other line of business. David Nutt has a good reputation here at the bank; I would say he is an honest man."

James had tools repaired by the blacksmith and felt he was a good man. James left the bank and walked to the blacksmith shop where he found David sitting in front of the building.

After some small talk, James asked, "Would you be interested in a partnership deal with me to buy and operate the mill? Mrs. Green is offering to sell the mill to me but I don't have the ready cash to buy it nor the available time to operate it."

"Mr. Furman, we have done some business, but I don't know you well enough to go into a partnership."

"I don't know you that well either, but I've heard good things about you and I think you're an honest man. Why don't you ask around about me?"

"Fair enough. What kind of a proposition do you have in mind?"

"Mrs. Green didn't state a price, only that she needed an income for the rest of her life. I do feel she'll ask a reasonable price. Whatever it turns out to be, I suggest we split it and that we split the time required to operate the mill." David wanted to think about it and said he would give James an answer before the week ended.

David was a single man and had homesteaded north of town but lost his claim during the financial downturn in 1893. He liked the sand hill country and had decided to stay. Since there was not a blacksmith in town and he had some experience in shoeing horses and repairing wagons, he thought he could make a living doing these things. He had been successful. Being younger than James and without a wife, his wants and needs were basic. This had allowed him to save some money.

True to his word, three days later he rode out to James and Belle's place to talk some more. "Belle, this is David Nutt, the man I was telling you about."

"Pleased to meet you, Mr. Nutt. Won't you stay for dinner?" After a good meal cooked by Belle, the two men discussed a financial arrangement to buy the mill. David spoke first. "I have some cash but not enough and I don't have anything to mortgage other than the old shed I work out of and that's not worth much. What can you put up?"

"David, can I call you that? We don't have much cash, but we do have land that can be used as collateral for a loan. We just don't want to mortgage the whole place." David seemed to be warming to the idea. He added, "I think the mill itself could be used as collateral. That should help."

They talked about splitting the time required to operate the mill so both could continue with their present work. Everything would be on a 50-50 arrangement. They shook hands and said they would meet at the bank the next day.

Later that night Belle said, "I heard you agree to mortgage our land again. James, I'm getting tired of you always putting us into debt. We are always scrimping, struggling, and saving every penny. When will you ever stop?"

"Belle, I did agree to mortgage part of our land, but not all of it. I don't like being in debt any more than you, but sometimes when opportunities occur you need to take advantage of them."

"I have heard that before!"

"Belle, look at what we have gained in the 13 years we have been here and think about what we have gone through to get where we are."

"That's just it. I don't want to repeat what we have gone through." The discussion continued for awhile, somewhat heated at times.

"Belle, it will all turn out for the best. We'll be better off, you'll see." They finally compromised, if part of the land would not provide enough money for their half, and then there would be no deal.

The next morning James rode into town and met David at the bank. The banker was willing to loan money on Furman land, but not on the mill itself. "You fellows must realize that two loans on one enterprise is not good business. The bank can't loan you money on the mill and the Furman land, too." The bank mortgage on one section of land, plus David's cash would leave them between $2,500 and $3,000 short. Leaving the bank the two men debated what to do. They both realized they were talking about a financial level higher than either one of them had ever experienced.

They talked about the possibilities of a good income from the mill. The country was growing: more people, more business, more people farming and raising cattle. All this should mean increased business for the mill. There were more trains carrying cattle and grain back east. That all sounded good.

On the other hand, they could lose everything they owned. A bad winter or a drought would mean almost no business. Then how could they pay back borrowed money? David did not want to be broke again, even though he did not have family to worry about. James did have family to provide for and the beginnings of a large ranch. David was ready to forget the whole thing. James considered the risk, but still being the optimist, he just knew everything would work out.

"David, let's talk to the widow about paying what we're short over a period of time. She said she was looking for steady income."

"I don't know. Maybe you have a good idea. I guess she can't do anymore than say no."

"David, what do you think about this: with the bank loan on our place and the cash you have, we could offer $3,000 down and about $300 per year for the next ten years?"

"That sounds fair to me. Let's see what she says to that offer." This was very acceptable to the widow, because it would give her an income for the next 10 years as well as a sizeable amount of cash.

James went home to tell Belle. "James, how in the world will the mill earn a profit large enough to pay $300 a year to Mrs. Green and then have enough left to split so that we can pay the bank loan?"

"Belle, the income from the mill should be $700 or more a year. That will leave $400 or more a year for David and us to split after the $300 payment was made to Mrs. Green. That, plus what we make from the sale of calves and grain should be enough to pay off the bank in five years or less." As always James was optimistic and Belle was doubtful. Buying the mill did prove to be a good move; but financial struggles still existed.

The Furman family had been getting new neighbors to the south and east the last five years. Since these families sent their children to the school Belle had started, they would cross the river near the school when they went to Rushville. A road of sorts was developing through the Furman property. Because of more people crossing the river at the same place, the river bottom was shifting, making the crossing less convenient. Another problem at the crossing was in the spring when the snows melted and heavy rains occurred. During these times, the

Niobrara would flood and widen with the current becoming stronger, which made the crossing somewhat hazardous. With the beginning of the new century, people wanted improvements in the river crossing. One day several families showed up at the Furman house to talk to James and Belle about building a bridge across the river.

James said, "Folks are always welcome to cross our land to get to town, but I hope you don't expect Belle and me to build and pay for a bridge." Most of the men said they would be willing to help build the bridge and a few said they would be willing to give some money to buy the lumber. But all expected James and Belle to provide most of the money and effort. "I agree our family would get the most good from a bridge since we own land on both sides of the river, but folks we just don't have the cash to build a bridge. We're already in debt and we cannot go into debt any further."

Then one man asked, "Do you think the County Commissioners would pay for it?" James responded, "It might have to be public land for the county to pay for it and we have no intention of giving any land to the county. That's asking too much."

Belle, in the meantime, was having a great time visiting with the ladies. They were talking about how they should get together occasionally. Recipes were being exchanged and the best way to can garden produce was being discussed. Baby announcements were the highlight of the conversation.

Once in awhile they would stop and listen in on what the men were discussing. When Belle heard James' response to the question of the county paying for a bridge, she walked over to James and made a suggestion. "Why don't some of you go talk to the Commissioners and see what they might be willing to do."

James thought for a minute then turned toward the others, "I'll be willing to do that if some of you fellows will go with me." All of those there said they would go and bring some of their neighbors with them.

At the next County Commissioners meeting about 20 men showed up surprising the Commissioners. This was the largest audience to attend a meeting since they discussed building a new school. After old business was taken care of, the committee wanted to know what they had on their minds. James stood up to speak, "We are requesting that a bridge be built over the Niobrara River near the school that is on our land. The river crossing is about washed out and during spring floods, people can't cross at all."

The Commissioners' first response was that the county could not pay for building bridges on private property. One commissioner said, "If we built this bridge, then every landowner on the river or on a stream would want the county to build a bridge on their land."

Charles Brown, who sat behind James, stood up and said, "The rest of us are not asking you to put a bridge on our lands, and we just want this one built." Bill Jansen then pointed out, "A bridge was needed to help the children cross the river to get to school." Charles chimed in, "This is the way many of us get to town and we can't do that when the river floods." Others voiced opinions as to why a bridge should be built over the river. A lot of heads were nodding and there was a low rumble from the crowd. The Commissioners thought a short recess to discuss the request would be good.

During the recess, the Commissioners differed over approving or denying the request. But since two of them were merchants in town, they could see lost sales chances if the people could not get to town. The third member asked where the county was going to get the money. True, the county had only limited funds and no labor force other than those men who worked for the county as a substitute tax payment.

Another thought was the number of voters they were facing on one hand, while on the other hand was the people that might view approval as favoritism. They decided they would postpone a decision until the next meeting. The men left not knowing whether they had succeeded or not. It would be another month until they knew. In the meantime several of the men decided to talk to the Commissioners privately, one on one.

During the next 30 days whenever one of the men was in town, they would remind the merchants that they would have not been there if the river had been in flood stage. Nor would their children have been able to go to school (never mind that the school term only lasted four months now). Word got around of their request to build a bridge but no one seemed to be objecting. All this effort had an effect on the Commissioners.

At the next meeting there were 20 men again in attendance. The Commissioners announced, "The County will pay for lumber for a bridge, but it would be up to you fellows to haul the lumber to the site and provide the labor to build the bridge. Also, there would be no reduction in the taxes of those who worked on the bridge. And one more thing, the bridge must be completed within one year. Mr. Furman, you are responsible for the project and are to report to the Commissioners on the building progress."

The men cheered and went to the tavern to celebrate. The Commissioners were invited to join them. In fact most of them celebrated too much. James had ridden to town in a wagon so he could bring back some supplies for the house and a roll of barbed wire. Instead he took six men who were too drunk to make it on their own to their homes. He left town in not too good of shape himself and with six horses tied on the back of his wagon. Others followed along on their own horses. Most of them weaving around in the saddle or hunched over with pale faces.

The first home he came to was Charles Brown's. He stopped the wagon near the front door and was helping Charles out when Mrs. Brown came out. When she saw her husband's condition, she verbally attacked both her husband and James.

At the next home James stopped the wagon about 100 yards away from the house, put the owner on his horse and sent the horse on its way. He did not want anymore tongue lashings. There would be several wives upset this night and James would have a mess to clean out of the wagon the next day.

After seeing all the men home, James went to his house. He stopped in front of the barn at about 10 o'clock. He hoped Belle would be in bed. He unhitched the horses, hung up the harnesses; and then splashed water from the trough on his face. Belle was in the kitchen when he walked in. "Well, what did the Commissioners say?"

James slurred, "They agreed to pay for the lumber for a bridge."

"James, you have been drinking!"

"We just had a little celebration."

"I think it was too much celebration. I am surprised. No – I am ashamed of you."

"I'm sorry. I guess I got carried away."

"Well, it's a good thing all the children are in bed."

"This is the first time I have been drunk and I swear it will be the last time."

CHAPTER 6
A TIME TO LOVE

During that first decade of the 20th century, the winters remained cold and snowy with a blizzard from time to time. The one advantage to winter was it provided ice. There was a spring-fed pond not far from the Furman ranch that would freeze deeply. Neighbors would gather there and cut big blocks of ice which they loaded on sleds and drug home. Most folks had a cellar or dugout where they would store the ice layered in straw or sawdust. If not disturbed often, the ice could last as long as mid-July.

The downside to this was that ice formed not only in the pond but also on the river. Then when it began to thaw in the spring the Furman children were assigned the task of breaking it up into small enough pieces so that it would not damage the bridge over the river as the ice floated down stream.

The summers were still hot and dry; however, there was usually sufficient rainfall for grass growth. So cattle prospered and hay could be cut and stacked for winter.

In the summer of 1904 a young man by the name of Edward Winston approached James with a question. "Mr. Furman, I would like to marry Edna. I'll take good care of her and treat her well. Will you give us permission to get married?"

Edward and Edna had met at a Saturday night dance in Rushville. They were attracted to one another and had been spending time together for five months.

"Edna is old enough to speak for herself. You don't need my permission. But I have a question for you. Do you like her or love her?"

"Both."

"Make sure you know the difference. Too many times a young buck thinks all there is to marriage is being in bed with a woman. How are you going to feel when you're broke, everything is going wrong, and she is yelling at you? Answer that question to yourself and you will know if you and Edna should get married."

That August the first Furman family marriage in Nebraska took place.

Also that year James finished acquiring another 980 acres and more debt. One day when he was in Rushville signing another loan to buy land he noticed an ad in the Rushville Recorder. It read:

Big Gala Day   Tuesday, September 13, 1904
Dedication of the New Court House
Special Speakers   Big Barbecue
Music by a Band   Races & Contests (prizes)
Bowery Dance all night
Don't miss the Greatest Event in the history of the County.

Prior to the new court house, all the county business had been conducted in a two story brick building owned by Mr. Hoyt. The lower level of the building was divided into rooms for county offices. The top floor was one large room where the district court was held. It was also used for Saturday night dances and as a theater on occasion.

James bought a newspaper and took it home for Belle to see. Belle thought it was a great idea to go. On Tuesday they left early in the wagon with the plan that the three young children could go to sleep in the wagon bed if they stayed late, which they did.

It was near nine o'clock when they left town, but with a full moon, seeing was no problem. The problem was Evan was nowhere to be found when they left and James was hopping mad!

"Now, James, calm down. Evan is 17 years old and should be able to take care of himself."

"That's not it. How is he going to get home? And if he does get home, he won't be worth a shit tomorrow."

"Don't swear in front of the children! And you are not going to be in much better shape yourself!"

Nothing else was said all the way home, even Ava and J.B. were quiet. About noon the next day Evan showed up on a borrowed horse. James was working in the barn. His anger swelled up again when he saw Evan. He picked up a horse halter and was going to beat Evan with it.

With the first swing Evan grabbed the halter and pulled it away from James. "I am as big as you are now, Pa, and your days of hitting me are over. I'm sorry if I caused you and Ma concern, but I'm going to start living my own life. That doesn't mean I'm walking out and leaving you. It means that I should be treated like a man. It also means that I should get some wages now."

James was taken aback. He turned and started walking away, then turned back again to face Evan. "I guess you're right. You are a man now and may be entitled to wages but I don't have money to pay you. Right now you get meals and a place to sleep. Guess I could give you a calf or two now and then. That's the best I can do for now."

"Agreed. Let's forget about last night and this morning."

In 1907 a recession developed and beef prices fell sharply. Income of the Furman family was reduced for the next three years. Making mortgage payments became a big problem. Somehow James managed to make each loan payment on time. At the same time black leg disease, which was fatal to many cattle, hit the area. Most ranchers believed it was spread by coyotes and wolves that had eaten an infected cow. James and the boys were of the same opinion. They always had a rifle with them and were on the lookout for both.

Evan continued to work for his father for another five years after their altercation. During this time he exercised his independence, sometimes too much. Like the time he had a little too much to drink in a saloon close to the Pine Ridge Indian Reservation. There was a young Indian there who had more than reached his limit. The two had a confrontation and punches were thrown. The Indian was too drunk to injure Evan and Evan was sober enough to realize he had better get out of there.

It wasn't long after that that Evan's attention turned toward a neighboring girl by the name of Milla Jackson. His time in saloons diminished and his time spent at the Jackson place increased. In the spring of 1909 Evan and Milla married and moved to a place of their own east of James and Belle, and closer to the Jackson's. Milla's parents gave them 320 acres as a wedding present and Evan had obtained some calves over the last five years, so the newlyweds had land and a small herd of cattle. They were a happy young couple hoping to be successful in starting a place of their own.

Both J.B. and Leo began doing chores at an early age. By the time J.B. was 12 and Leo, 10, they stopped going to school because they were needed to do the many things required to provide for the family livelihood.

Leo was responsible for feeding and watering the horses before he could go to school. Feeding was not that much of a problem but taking them to the river to drink was. All of them were at least 10 times bigger than Leo and some of them had a mind of their own. So Leo usually took them one at a time and still had trouble sometimes. But even if there were no problems, by the time he had completed his assignment every morning it was too late to go to school, so he just quit. J.B. also had found school interfering too much with his tasks and had dropped out of school also.

The summer Leo was 14 he was to inspect the fences and check the cattle once a month. On one trip his horse slipped and fell on Leo, breaking his leg. The horse got up; Leo couldn't, but he did get to his knees. A man on his hands and knees seemed to spook the horse, which ran off. Leo was at least a mile from the house. He crawled and drug himself all the way back to the house.

Right outside the yard fence he yelled with what strength he had left. "Help!....Mom...Help!"

Belle looked out and saw her boy lying in the dirt. She ran out. "Leo, what has happened?"

After one look, Belle sent Ava to town for the doctor. She knew Leo's leg was broken, but it was also scratched and bloody; she did not want to try to set it herself. J.B. came by the house about that time, so Belle and J.B. carried Leo into the house and cut off his pants. Belle told J.B. to find James and tell him what happened. She then washed Leo's leg and gave him some laudanum for the pain.

It was nighttime when the doctor got there. He was able to set the bone but infection had already set in. He told James and Belle, "Leo needs to go to a hospital. The best one I know of is in Omaha. I suggest you get him there." The next morning, while Belle stayed home with the other children, James and Leo left on the train for Omaha. Leo sang all the way.

Leo was admitted and James stayed with him a day and a half. James was told Leo would need to stay for 10 days or until the infection cleared up, otherwise Leo might lose his leg. "Leo, how would you feel about staying here 10 days by yourself?"

"It would be OK. They're nice to me and the food is good. But I don't have anything to do." James went out and bought Leo a book and a bag of candy. He then returned to the hospital.

"Leo, your mom or I will be back in eight or nine days and we'll take you home. Try to do what they tell you." James returned nine days later and Leo was released from the hospital. His leg never returned to normal but Leo never let it slow him down.

It was during this time that the doctor stopped by. "Belle, Charles Brown's daughter has diphtheria and I think his wife may be coming down with it, too. Could you look in on them for the next few days?" Belle gladly said she would. It was not the first time she had stepped in when a serious illness occurred. A year before she had gone over to

John Tinnin's place when three of his children had scarlet fever. She looked after them until their fever broke.

"Ava, find your Pa and tell him I'm going over to the Brown's. They have diphtheria, so don't go there. I'll be back in a week if they're well enough to get around." Ava assumed the cooking and washing chores until her mother returned.

By the end of 1908 James and Belle had acquired 3,200 acres including Mary Pearl's land, and they had a growing cattle herd.

Mary Pearl had bought a house in Rushville and moved the summer of 1909. To Leona this was the right time to talk to her parents about going to high school. During supper one summer night she announced, "I would like to go to high school and now that Grandma is living in town I could stay with her."

"James, what do you think?"

"I don't see why not. Mother would probably like to have someone with her."

"I would have liked for Edna and Evan to have gone to high school, but that never happened. Now J.B. and Leo will never make it, so at least you girls can go."

"Belle, Edna and Evan are doing all right for themselves and I'm sure J.B. and Leo are going to be alright too. They read and write, as well as have a good level head on their shoulders."

That fall Leona enrolled in Rushville High School and spent the winter with Mary Pearl. She would do so for the next four years. Leona and Mary Pearl developed a loving relationship during the four years she attended high school.

The winter of 1909-10 was long and cold. Many times that winter the Furman family was snowbound. Getting hay to the cattle was almost an impossibility. It would take two teams of horses to move sleds loaded with hay. Usually one team would break a trail through the snow, and then the other team would struggle to drag the sled forward. Usually additional shoveling was needed as well.

The daily life of caring for animals, repairing fences, and stacking hay continued for the Furman men. Weeding the garden, cooking and canning, washing and everything else continued for Belle and the girls.

By 1910 both boys had become expert riders and capable of doing a man's work. Actually they were doing most of the work and James was becoming more of an overseer.

One early October day the two boys were moving the cattle from the south place to the north place, so the herd would be all in one place. The calves were to be cut out and moved to the railroad for marketing. When they finished moving the cattle, J.B. asked Leo what he wanted to do for the rest of his life. Leo gave J.B. a funny look and said, "I just want to raise cattle."

"You can't be serious! What about going some place and seeing things?"

"J.B., I like where we live and I'm happy doing what we do. I don't have any desire to leave here or do anything else."

"Not me. I want to go places and try different things. When I get enough money I'll try doing something besides moving cattle, branding cattle, and feeding cattle. I get tired of cattle."

"If I were you, I wouldn't tell Pa that. He's starting to let us do about everything around here. It wouldn't surprise me if he and Ma didn't move into town before too many more years. Both of them talk about it."

"Pa won't stay in town. He might sleep there some, but he couldn't handle town living."

A week later the steers were penned up. Their neighbor, Charles Brown, had also penned his steers up. The Furman's and the Brown's combined their steers for a drive to the railroad pens in Rushville. To-gether they moved 500 steers. The day of the drive began early with the two groups meeting a mile north of the Furman ranch. One older steer had a bell around his neck and Leo got him started and rode point. Jay rode on one side of the herd and James on the other. Charles and his son pushed up from the rear.

The move was uneventful, possibly because of the decision to not go through town, but around it. It was late afternoon when they reached the pens at the railroad. The cattle buyer had gone home. He was not happy because he had to return to the railroad pens, and James was concerned that a fair price would not be offered. The offer made seemed acceptable to both James and Charles. There would not have been anything they could have done if the offer had been unacceptable. The steers were already in the pen.

By the end of 1910 the ranch was composed of over 4,060 acres, over six sections. However, it was not adjacent. There was a separation, which they began to call the north place and the south place. James continued to buy land and mortgage land, buy land and mortgage land. Each time there was a heated debate with Belle. There came a time when the debt became too great, he had to sell his part of the ownership in the mill to pay off the loans.

A fair-sized herd of Black Angus had been acquired as well as several head of horses, which they were now raising and selling.

The Furman name was well respected in the cattle and farming circles. Floyd Peck, the Rushville farm implement dealer, asked James if he could use his name in an advertisement for the new *Endless Apron Spreader*. James had recently purchased one to haul manure away from the barn. Mr. Peck thought if he listed James name along with some other prominent men, it would influence others to buy. James was always ready to try the newest and latest pieces of equipment.

"I'm not sure my name is going to sell anything, but I have no objection to you putting it in you're ad. Besides I may need a favor from you sometime."

"I won't forget and I'll give you a good deal the next time you buy something from me."

"Don't know of anything I need right now."

"You'll probably be interested in something before long. There are improvements and new things coming along all the time now. Just last month they started telephone service in Rushville. I even have a telephone in our business place now."

"I know. The last time I was in town I saw one of the new automobiles. If I were going into a business, I would sell those things."

At a July 4, 1912 dance, Ava met a young man by the name of James Finn. A love relationship developed and the following February they were married. James Finn had homesteaded 160 acres east of the Furman's. He had completed his homestead obligation just before he married Ava. Shortly after their marriage, he was able to buy another 120 acres. Four years after their marriage the couple decided to sell their place to James and Belle and they moved to Newcastle, Wyoming. At Ava's wedding ceremony, J.B. met Iva Roberts and a year later he approached James with a proposition.

"Pa, I found a girl I'd like to marry. The problem is I don't have a house or any income. Before Evan left you agreed to provide him a bed and food and you gave him six calves a year. The old house is still good and it's empty. I would like to live there and work for you for wages or land or cattle."

"So you think you'd like to get married? Are you ready to quit going to town for drinking? Are you ready to be responsible for someone other than yourself?"

"Yes, I am, Pa. I know that I'll need to do things different now. Funny thing is what used to seem important to me doesn't seem as important now."

"I guess it is time for you to be your own man and if marriage is what you want, do it. You can have the old house and we'll work out something money-wise so you can get married. That is—if Iva will have you."

"Thanks, Pa. Now I can ask Iva to marry me. Guess now I need to think about furniture and stuff. Pa, did you talk to Evan like this when he got married?"

"Yes I did, probably more so because he was planning to move to his own place. I hate to see you boys grow up and start leaving the ranch."

"I'm not leaving you, Pa."

"We're going to need more land and raise more calves if there is going to be two families living on this place."

"Pa, I remember hearing that Tom Murray wanted to sell some of his land. We could talk to him."

"Alright, in the morning we'll ride over to his place and see if we can make a deal."

A deal was made to buy 480 acres and another loan was obtained from the bank. But this time there were two names on the contract:

James and J.B. Furman. The deal included a two-story cement block house that was only a year old, as well as some other buildings.

In April, J.B. and Iva Roberts were married. After the wedding ceremony as James and Belle left the church, James said, "You feeling alright, Belle?"

"I'm just tired, I guess. It's so hard anymore to keep the house and garden. And with all the children beginning to leave and get married, I just feel old."

"Maybe you need someone to help you. There's a young girl staying with the Cooper's that might be willing to help you."

"I don't know, I'll think about it. James, have you ever thought about moving into town?"

"I suppose we will some day, but I'm not ready yet."

Belle was not the only one bothered by aging problems.

In 1913, a month before graduation, Leona walked into Mary Pearl's house and found her dead from a heart attack. Leona was devastated. "Why did Grandma die?" she kept asking.

"Leona, we all must die sometime. Dying is just as much a part of life as being born." James did his best to console her. Belle, although not really sorry Mary Pearl was gone, did a better job of comforting Leona.

The 420 acres Mary Pearl had accrued was to be divided among her six children. However, since none of them lived nearby, they were more than willing to sell their share to James and Belle.

In the spring of 1914 Belle became sick. James went over to the Cooper's place on Deer Creek and asked Mrs. Cooper's niece, Edith Hart, if she would be interested in a job of helping his wife. She was interested since she had no source of income and had been living with her aunt and uncle for almost a year. "I can't pay very much but you will have a place to stay and food to eat as well as some money. I will send one of our boys over to get you and your things tomorrow."

The next morning James assigned Leo the task of going over to get Edith. Leo felt a little nervous about this but didn't complain. He liked being around the young girls, especially at the dances he had attended. There wasn't much conversation between the two as Leo drove the buggy back; Edith did most of what talking took place.

After Edith moved in, Leo seemed to change. He was more willing to help around the house and found excuses to be at the house. When the family went anyplace or when Leo heard about a dance, Edith went and was always near Leo.

Early that December as James, J.B. and Leo were taking hay out to feed cattle, Leo said, "Pa, I want to marry Edith."

"I'm not surprised. The way you have been hanging around her. Tell me though, just how are you going to provide for her?"

"I was in hopes I could work for you like J.B. does."

"Where would you live? You don't have a house."

J.B. came to Leo's rescue. "Pa, I know you and Ma have been thinking about moving into town. This might be a good time to do that. Leo and I can run things around here and you and Ma can start taking things easy."

"So you think I'm too old to do anything?"

"I'm not saying that Pa, but I can tell it is harder for you to do some things and Ma needs things easier. If you did move to town, Leo could live in the stone house on the north place."

"Well, I've got to confess; your mother and I have been talking about moving into town. It's just I am not sure I can handle being cooped up in town."

"You don't have to stay in town all the time. Come back out here whenever you want to, everyday if you want."

"Well, if we're going to have a three-way split, we're going to need room to run more cattle. I'll see if we could lease the school land section. That would allow us to handle another 50 or 60 cows. That should put us at close to a 600 cow herd. Maybe that would be enough for the three of us. You boys have been doing just about everything already, so maybe it is time. I'll talk to your ma tonight."

James and Belle found a house for sale in Rushville. Belle was happy. She could go to church every Sunday now, something she was not able to do while they were on the ranch.

"James, I sure missed going to church while we lived on the ranch."

"I can't deny that being with a group of good people once a week does make me feel good. But I always knew there was a God. I could see him every time I stood on a hill and looked around. Don't think I have to go to a building to see God."

"Knowing there is a God is not enough James. You need to really know him—personally, and that will happen if you continue to listen to people telling about God in their lives."

J.B. and Iva moved into the stone house at Leo's insistence because they were older and had been married longer. Leo and Edith went to Chadron to be married and have a short honeymoon. They were married on December 23rd and Leo always said it was the best Christmas present he ever received. They moved into the house near the river on the south place.

Edith & Leo

James and Belle settled into town living. Belle adjusted better than James. To James, everything seemed too close and confining. That spring there was a lot of excitement in Rushville. Electricity came to town; a big ceremony took place that summer when Main Street was lighted for the first time. In the fall James and Belle had electric lights in their house. James had to admit it was something he could not have obtained on the ranch.

Life was a little easier for James and Belle in town. Belle liked having neighbors to visit with and being able to walk to a store whenever she wanted. James was friendly with the neighbors, but spent a lot of time going back and forth to the ranch.

CHAPTER 7
A Time to Weep

The winter of 1914-15 was not only cold; there was more snow than usual. Evan's wife, Milla, was expecting their fourth child and J.B.'s wife, Iva, was expecting their first child. Belle was very concerned about both of them because they were so far from town and it was the middle of winter. "James, you need to go get Iva and Milla and bring them into our house in case a doctor's needed when the babies arrive. There's no way a doctor could get to them when the time comes."

"As much snow as there is on the ground, I don't know if I could get to them. Maybe the snow will melt some, and then I could go after them."

"Can't wait long, Milla is due in five weeks and Iva is not that far behind her."

A week later the sun came out. James decided to try for Evan's place first since it was not that far off a road trail. He got two neighbors to ride their horses through the snow in front of his buggy. Still they had to free the buggy when the snow was too deep. It took seven hours to reach Evan's house. The next day they made the return trip to town in less time.

It snowed that night but the sun came out again the next day and James thought it was time to try to reach Iva. There was not much of a road to follow, so James followed the hilltops where the snow had partially blown away. From time to time he would have to stop and take down the barbed wire, go across, and then put it back in place. Only one valley had to be crossed and there the snow had to be dug out, still it was an all day trip. Again the return trip took less time. The trip had been hard on both expectant mothers, but they were safely in Rushville.

Milla went into labor on February 14th. Belle sent James after Evan. Things did not go well. The doctor was able to deliver a healthy girl; however, Milla hemorrhaged and the doctor could not stop the bleeding. Milla died. Evan was stunned. He could not believe his wife was gone. He walked out the door into the snow totally in a daze. James went after him with a coat, which he got on him after some effort.

Both men just sat in the snow. "Evan, I know you loved your wife and this is hard for you right now, but you must go on. Life is for the living and you now have four kids to take care of."

"How am I going to do that, Pa? Jim is only six and the two girls four and three. I can't cook or sew. How am I going to care for them? I can't nurse a baby. What am I going to do?"

"You will find a way; just don't lose control of your thinking. As for the baby, I know Ma will want to care for her until she is older or you are ready for her. Let's go back to the house."

"Not just yet. You go on back. I'll be back before long."

"OK, but stay out of the saloon, you don't need a drink."

When Evan did return, Belle asked, "What do you want to name your new daughter?" It took Evan a few minutes to realize a name had not been discussed and now there was no one to discuss it with. "She should have her mother's name since she cannot have a mother."

There was still a heavy cloud over the house when Iva went into labor. James went after J B.

The doctor came again and this time the birth went without a problem. On March 1st Iva delivered a baby girl. The girl was healthy but

Iva was exhausted after the birth. Iva and J.B. thought the girl should be named after her grandmother, Helen Isabelle.

Then 15 days later trouble visited the house again. Iva began having problems breathing. Her lungs filled with fluid and on March 19, she died. Belle would have two babies to care for. There was never a doubt in Belle or James mind as to what needed to be done nor who would do it. Two funerals took place that spring and two brothers grieved. The rest of the family grieved with them. Two mothers dying within a month was a heavy burden to bear. Tragedy would return to the family again two years later.

Evan soon started a search for someone to help raise his children and take care of his house. He found help in Mary Irene Buskirk whom he hired and later married in the fall. J.B. would remain single for 20 years. Little Milla went home to live with her father and new mother. Baby Helen Isabelle would remain under her grandmother and grandfather's roof until she was grown.

In May 1915 the Germans torpedoed the Lusitana and the newspapers were full of stories of a war in Europe and should the United States go to war or not. In Rushville it all seemed so very far away and unimportant. The boys and James discussed what was happening in Europe. The events were just not a part of their everyday lives. Cattle prices were favorable and the Furman's were prosperous. Then in March 1917 three unarmed American ships were sunk without any warning. There were many lives lost. On April 4, 1917 the United States declared war against Germany.

The war was about to become part of their lives. "Leo, did you hear about Tom Murray joining the Army?"

"Yea, J.B., I heard about it. I wasn't surprised; he always said he would leave here if he got the chance. You plan on joining?"

"No, Pa needs me here since you took sick. I have to do your work and mine, too."

"Don't make it sound like I'm not doing anything. I just get tired sometimes; can't help it. Let's change the subject. What do you think about the women getting to vote for some of the government office holders?"

"I think the politicians are just staying in the middle of the road and trying to please everybody. They think they've pleased some folks by passing the law to allow women to vote for some offices. Then the rest of those that are against women voting feel better about women not being able to vote for all office holders. Me, I just think if the women are going to get to vote, then they should get to vote for all office holders."

"I don't know if Edith will vote or not, but I bet Ma will."

"Well, I don't have a wife, so I am staying out of any discussion about it."

On May 18, 1917 congress passed the Selective Service Act that required all males between the ages of 21 and 31 to register for possible induction into the military. In June, Evan, J.B. and Leo reported to the draft board in Rushville. Evan went first.

"Name?"

"Evan Justin Furman."

"Married or single?"

"Widower with four kids."

"Age?"

"I'll be 31 on the first of July."

"Mister, stay and raise your kids. We don't need men bad enough to take you."

When it was J.B.'s turn, he stepped forward and heard the usual question, "Your name?" He answered, "J.B." "Is that spelled Jay?"

"No, it's just the letter J."

"You can't use just your initials. What is your first name?"

"J.B. is all I have ever been called. That is the only name I have."

"Well, from now on its first name J-a-y and middle initial B." He was classified 1A. Leo was next and it was obvious he was not well. He had come down with scarlet fever in May. Between that and his bad leg, he was classified as unacceptable for military service.

When he got home, Leo told Edith, "They told me I was unacceptable for the army. That bothers me to think of myself that way, but I'm glad that I won't have to leave you."

"Oh, so am I, Leo. With the baby coming I want you here. Belle and James already have two babies at their house; I can't impose on them. Now I can birth the baby here and feel secure knowing you're nearby."

In mid-July Leo started staying close to the house. Belle's youngest daughter, Mary came out to stay with Edith and Leo that summer. She was a great help to Edith. Having another female around made Leo feel better. He had delivered many calves and colts; however, human babies were an entirely different matter.

When Edith started having labor pains, Leo saddled a horse and went to get Mrs. Riggs, their neighbor to the west, for help. Ira was born on July 16th. Edith had no problems in the delivery and Leo was a proud new father.

Three mornings later Edith went to Ira's crib and found him dead. Leo heard the scream from the house and ran from the barn. Edith and Mary were on the floor sobbing while Edith rocked the dead baby. Many months passed before life returned to both Edith and Leo.

Edith put all of her energy into trying to keep busy. She did not want to think about Ira. She worked in the garden longer than necessary. Then canned and dried everything she could find. She made enough soap to last five years. Killed and cleaned a chicken every day. Leo soon got tired of chicken. "Kill a steer then and I'll cure and can the meat."

"You need to slow down. You've churned plenty of butter and made more cottage cheese than we can eat. I know you want to keep your mind off Ira, but you're going to make yourself sick. I need you and you need me. We just have to keep going. We're young and I know there will be other children."

Edith did try to slow down – so to speak, but civilization seemed to be moving on. There were electric lights in town, women could vote in a limited way, and now if a man wanted a drink of whiskey he had to go to South Dakota or Wyoming. The Furman men began to wonder what was going to happen next. They didn't have to wait long.

The message: *Greetings and salutations. You have been chosen by your fellow Americans,* came for Jay B. in early November. He was to report for duty at the U.S. Navy recruiting Station, Omaha, Nebraska no later than 12 December 1917. Jay reported and was sent to the Great Lakes Training base. After basic he was assigned to the battleship, U.S.S. Indiana, as a fireman. He went to sea three times. His pay was $41.00 per month, $15.00 was sent to his daughter, Helen, and $6.70 was taken out for insurance.

The war ended November 11, 1918 but Jay still had three years and one month left on his enlistment. In February Jay requested release from service due to having a motherless child and parents whose health was failing, which made it difficult to maintain their ranch. This was a bit of a stretch but the navy had more men than they needed, so his request was granted on May 1, 1919. Jay left Brooklyn, New York for Rushville. Jay never regretted his navy service but he said, "The only waves I want to see from now on is the waving of blowing grass."

Leo helped him reopen the stone house and the partnership resumed. One day while they were cleaning up the house, Leo asked, "What were the big cities like?"

"A lot of people. Houses are right next to each other and some people live on top of one another in the same building. They don't even have room to breathe. Everybody always seems to be in a hurry – going or coming from someplace. Be glad you don't live there."

"Doesn't sound like anyplace I would want to live."

While Jay had been in service, James and Leo had bought another half section and increased the size of the herd. Once again there was a mortgage to pay.

Leo and Edith had another son born just before Jay returned home. He was named Lyle. Both mother and father were very protective of their second son. This time the baby grew and was walking by the time he was a year old.

James had started thinking about going into some business in town. Jay and Leo both encouraged him to sell automobiles. "Dad, there are automobiles everywhere back east and it won't be long before the same is true out here."

"Jay is right. Look at the way the Ford place has grown in the short time they've been in business."

"What do I know about automobiles? I've never even been in one."

"You know about threshing machines and all kinds of farm equipment. Automobiles are the same thing, only they have motors on them."

"I did see an article in the paper about somebody traveling around wanting to establish a place to sell an automobile called a REO. I could talk to him and hear what he has to say, but I don't remember when he was going to be in Rushville."

"I remember seeing that article, too. I think it was last Tuesday and the man's name was Stewart."

"Enough of this, boys. We have calves to brand and castrate and we're a month behind in this job. It should've been done in April. Rope another one, Leo." Leo roped each calf; Jay wrestled it to the ground and tied it up. James then applied the branding iron. As he did so the top prong on one side of the iron broke off. "I'm getting tired of these top prongs cracking and breaking off. Ever time we brand we run into this same problem. The metal will only bend one way so maybe that's what we should use. Then we won't always be rewelding a piece to the top of the rail end."

"You have a good thought, Pa. I know I get tired of repairing these irons."

"I agree with Jay. Let's change the brand from the anchor F to the rocking F. I don't know of anyone else using that mark."

"From now on when one of these prongs break off, I'm just going to keep using the iron and when we make new branding irons, we'll just bend the ends down."

James was thinking that waiting for Jay to get home before doing the branding was a mistake. It would take another long day to complete the task and then the calves would need to be moved to the south place.

Moving cattle across the river

Branding Time

On Tuesday morning Belle told James, "You might as well go see the REO man. You've been talking about it for three days now."

"I know. I just need something to do. But trying to sell automobiles is a lot different than running the mill. Besides, I don't know what kind of money a person would need to start selling automobiles."

"Well, go find out."

James went over to the hotel where the man was staying. He found other men were talking to Mr. Stewart. Most of them just seemed to be curious about automobiles and how much they cost. All of them were hoping for a ride in the one parked in front of the hotel. There was one man that James had never met nor seen before. He said his name was Ralph Gunther and he was from Chadron. He thought he might try selling in Rushville and if that worked out, he would start an agency in Chadron.

Mr. Stewart gave a convincing talk about the REO and how it was superior to other automobiles, telling how they had been manufactured since 1905. "Why, in the second year of selling them total sales was over $4.5 million." It all sounded very positive to James.

After the lookers drifted away, James and Ralph started asking specific questions. "Does the manufacturer send the automobiles out and we sell them, and then split the money?"

"No, a beginning agent buys three cars outright for an agreed price, and then he is free to sell them for whatever price he wants. After he sells three, he can get up to six more at a time and doesn't have to pay the manufacturer for four months. The agent does have to pay the shipping costs at the time of delivery. The manufacturer will also teach one mechanic to repair them, after you've sold 20 cars.

"What about a building and operating expenses?"

"That's to be provided by the agent. But the manufacturer does send out advertising posters and will help pay for newspaper advertising. As for the building, you need at least 3,000 square feet, 5,000 would be even better."

"You said the agent buys the first three cars outright. How much would three automobiles cost?"

"$2,800 will buy one touring automobile, one roadster, and one Z model. Selling those three should bring you a $400 to $500 profit, maybe more. Are either one of you interested in being an agent here in Rushville?"

Both James and Ralph answered yes. "Then maybe the two of your should consider going into partnership since there can only be one agency."

"How about it, Mr. Furman, would you agree on a partnership? You live here and know everyone and I have been selling things all my life."

"No offense, Mr. Gunther, but I don't know you. I would like to know you better before I answer that question."

Mr. Stewart said, "I'll be in town for two more days. Why don't you two get to know one another better and then come and see me before I leave?"

James took Ralph Gunther home for supper that night and they talked until late into the night. The next morning they met again. James could see that Gunther was a salesman and he seemed to be an upright man, yet there was something about him that bothered James. He was just not sure what it was. Belle was no help when he asked her what she thought of Ralph Gunther. Before Mr. Stewart left, Furman and Gunther signed an agreement with the REO manufacturing company to be their agent in Rushville, Nebraska.

Ralph put up $1,400 which he said he could make available after returning to the Chadron bank. James went to the bank to mortgage part of the ranch for his $1,400. James soon realized he had gotten himself financially deeper than he planned. There was no building available for the business. The only option was to build a building. James went to the bank again for another loan. The garage was built on the edge of town and REO's began to appear on the streets, but slowly. The new venture occupied all of James' time. A trip out to the ranch was rare.

Reo garage & Reo car

On the ranch Leo and Jay were digging wells with a spade and a bucket. James made suggestions about where to dig, but never helped with the work. Water for the cattle was needed at both the north and south ranges. After the holes got too deep for a ladder, they attached a pulley to a three-legged log frame and used a horse to raise dirt and lower shovels and a person. After finding water, which sometimes was more than 100 feet below the ground level, they would build a windmill to pump the water to the surface.

Windmills had improved the last few years. There was an oil reserve in the gear box which meant less maintenance. The cost could be kept to less than $400 per windmill, if they did all the work. Leo and Jay thought it was a good investment. The cattle did not have to rely on the river for water. They had had windmills at both houses for 15 years, but these were the first on the open land.

Leo thought it was time to buy one of those new tractors. He told Jay, "We should buy a tractor. They say it'll last longer than a horse and you don't have to feed it."

"I've been thinking about the same thing. After all, Pa's selling automobiles and is even driving one now."

"Do you know how much one would cost?"

"No, but it shouldn't cost any more than an automobile. Surely we can come up with that much money."

They purchased a new Case tractor for $1,090. The timing was not good for Jay and Leo, neither for James in automobile sales. Inflation of more than 15% started in 1919 and continued through 1920. Then the economy went into a recession. Even though that only lasted for two years, Jay and Leo suffered and almost lost their tractor but they were able to borrow more money to keep going.

For James it was worse. Not only were the Reo's not selling, Ralph Gunther left town with what cash they had. There were bills James could not pay. He sold the building and returned the automobiles he could. What he could not return he sold at a loss. Belle and James even had to sell their house in town. They moved back into the stone house with Jay on the north place. James was broke and bitter. He had never failed before. No longer would he have an optimistic outlook; even his personality seemed to change.

Though the recession was causing hardships, 1921 started out in a very positive way for Edith and Leo. On the first day of January, Amy was born. Mild weather allowed the doctor to be at the ranch for the birth. Both Edith and Amy did well. Now Lyle had a sister and life seemed good.

"Edith, we may not have any money, but we have our health and two wonderful kids. I am so happy."

"Oh, I am too, Leo."

Little Lyle would look at Amy; touch her, and then run away laughing.

CHAPTER 8

A Time to Mourn and a Time to Dance

L ater that year trouble came again. Lyle began having stomach pains. Edith's concern increased after two days of no change. "Leo, you must get the doctor to come out to examine Lyle. I don't think he's up to going into town." Leo didn't need any convincing. He saddled his horse and left immediately for Rushville. The doctor and Leo returned in the doctor's automobile.

"I'm not sure what's wrong with Lyle, but I believe he has appendicitis. I could operate; however, I know you have lost one son, so you may want to take him to the hospital in Omaha. The doctors there will know more than I do."

"How hard would such a trip be for him?"

"The worst part would be the ride into town. The train ride shouldn't bother him."

Since it was nighttime the doctor stayed with Edith and Leo. No one got much sleep that night, and there was a lot of discussion. When morning came the decision was made to go to the hospital in Omaha. Leo hitched a team to the wagon and Edith put a featherbed and blankets in it. Leo drove while Edith sat on the floor of the wagon bed with Lyle's head in her lap. Amy was in her mother's arms. The doctor followed in his automobile. Leo went slowly across the prairie watching for any possible hazards. Lyle made the trip without any additional pain. They got to town in time to board the train. Leo wrapped a blanket around Lyle and laid him across two seats. Edith cried as they left and felt so hopeless. She spent the night with Belle and James.

"Are you alright, Lyle?"

"Yes, Papa."

"We should be at the Omaha hospital tomorrow morning. If the pain comes back, tell me and I'll give you some of the medicine the doctors sent with me."

"I will, Papa."

"When I was a young boy my father took me on the train to the Omaha Hospital because I broke my leg. Your Grandpa told me to be strong and everything would turn out right. He was right. In the hospital the nurses were so nice to me and always got me something to eat when I was hungry."

Lyle made the trip without any complications. At the Omaha hospital the doctors confirmed the diagnosis of appendicitis. They removed Lyle's appendix but he did not get better. On November the 4th he died. Leo cried. How could he tell Edith? He tried to form the right words in his mind as he walked to the telegraph office. He sent two messages, one to Edith, and the other to James and Belle. Then Leo made the arrangements to take Lyle's body back to Rushville. Now there would be two Furman boys in the cemetery.

Jay happened to be in town when the telegrams arrived. He took one to James and left for the ranch with the other one. When Edith learned of Lyle's death, she went to the pine tree grove and fell on the ground crying, "Why, Lord?" There was no answer. As soon as Belle read the telegram she left for the ranch to console Edith. She knew where to find Edith. The same place she had gone when crushed by despair, the pine trees. "Edith, you must be strong. You have a beautiful baby girl to care for and raise. Think about her. I can't tell you why you've lost two boys. But you do have a girl that is going to need you and you are young enough to have another son."

"I know – but to lose two sons is too much! You never lost any children. How can you know how I feel?"

"I can't, Edith. Still I know it's hard for you. Try to remember, the living are still here and they need you."

The entire Furman family was at the station when the train arrived. Leo wrapped his arms around Edith and they cried together. No words were spoken. They just stood with arms around one another while Lyle's body was removed from the box car. Then they went directly from the train to the cemetery and buried Lyle next to his brother, Ira.

Not much was said that night at the house by the river, nor did anyone feel like eating. Edith nursed Amy and put her to bed. Leo just sat and stared into space. The next morning Edith said, "Leo, I want another son." Leo was surprised. He had been thinking what he could have done differently. His only answer was what if we had an automobile. Would that have made a difference?

Edith again turned to work to keep her mind off Lyle's death. It was winter so she could not work in the garden or do any canning, but she made soap again and again. She made cottage cheese. There was a pan of milk on the back of the cook stove clabbering every day. She sewed dresses for Amy. She crocheted and made quilts.

Leo kept his grief inside, but many times he would just stare into space. He seemed lost. The winter was mild that year with only normal snowfalls, and no cows were lost. This was a blessing. Neither Leo nor Edith could have handled any more ordeals. Slowly life returned. As the New Year began, Edith was pregnant and on September 2, 1922 Lloyd was born. The heaviness of the parent's hearts was lifted. Both Edith and Leo vowed nothing would happen to this son!

Lloyd was a child of hope. Not only for the healing of broken hearts, but also financial conditions began to change for the Furman's. Shortly after Lloyd's birth, the price for beef started to rise. Debts of both James and those of the ranch began to be satisfied. There was rain in both the spring and summer. The hay crop did well and no calves were lost. A feeling of optimism returned to Edith and Leo. "Edith, I think we should buy an automobile."

"You can't be serious. There's no road to the house. How are you going to get from here to town?"

"We can follow the wagon path. Besides, Dad says you can drive them across the grass lands as long as you watch out for drop offs and sharp rises."

"Well, where are you going to get the money?"

"We should have some extra money after we sell the steers this fall."

"Buying an automobile is up to you, Leo. I can get along without one."

"Edith, I always wondered if we had had an automobile, would Lyle still be alive. And now, what if Amy or Lloyd gets sick? That's why I think we should buy one."

"When you put it like that, how could I not agree?"

They bought a four-door Ford automobile.

Amy was growing and Lloyd was a healthy baby. During warm weather when the windows were open, Edith could tell when Leo was coming. Even before he got close to the house she could hear him whistling. All seemed right with the world.

One day when Leo was at the bank paying on a loan, he lost his composure. The small talk with the young man at the bank was about ranching. The young man said, "There's nothing to ranching. Just turn the cows out to pasture and later round them up, sell them, and cash the check."

Leo's eyes became like steel and his face reddened. "How would you like to work all summer in the boiling sun to get hay and feed for the winter? Then in the winter comes a whining, raging blizzard and there are 15 to 20 calves born and about to be frozen stiff in less than a day. You struggle to carry them to the barn and, if there is no room in the barn, you take them into your house. Sometimes you put them in a tub of warm water. Sometimes you put them in front of your stove in the house. Then you nurse them and when it's time to return them to their mother, you work to get an uncooperative cow to remember it's her calf!"

"I'm sorry. I just never stopped to think about what might be involved in raising cattle."

"I haven't told you half of the work in raising cattle. Young man, on any subject, you need to find out about it before you start making comments."

"Yes, sir. Please take no offense. I'm sorry"

"It's alright, just think before you talk."

In the summer of 1923 Belle and James' youngest daughter, Mary, married Robert Evans. Robert was a railway fireman and was gone quite a bit. One year after their marriage, Mary was pregnant and Robert was killed under mysterious circumstances at Norfolk, Nebraska. She moved in with Belle and James. Her son was born two months later.

Edith was also pregnant again and in February, 1925 Robert Earl was born. Edith and Leo were thrilled to have two sons and a daughter. Again life seemed good.

Leo realized that three children would require a lot of washing clothes. He bought Edith a washing machine that had a gasoline motor. She was so pleased but Leo soon felt it was a mistake. Every time Edith washed, Leo had to start the balky motor. He would stomp on the motor pedal over and over until it finally started. By then Leo was smoking as much as the motor.

On days that Amy and Lloyd could not go out due to the weather conditions, Edith would play "I spy" games with them. She also helped them learn the letters of the alphabet by using the name on the wood burning cook stove, Great Majestic. M was for mother, A was for Amy, J was for Uncle Jay, E was for Edith, S was for the dog, Spike, T was for teacher and I and C were for ice cream.

As 1926 began, Robert developed whooping cough. After three days the worrying parents could take no more. They had tried everything they knew to try. Leo went to town for the doctor but they did not get back to the ranch in time.

The evening of February 23, 1926 Robert died in Edith's arms. He only lived one year and three days. The blow was more than Edith could endure. After the funeral she went to bed and would not get up.

Losing three sons was more grief than any mother should experience. She prayed for her own death. Leo tried to comfort her, but in his own grief, did not offer much encouragement. Even Amy was affected. She could not understand why Robert was not there. Leo told her Robert had gone to be with God.

Then Lloyd got sick. Leo did not know how to tell Edith, but tell her he must. In the morning he walked into the bedroom and simply said, "Lloyd is sick and he needs you." Edith opened her eyes and thought for a minute, then said, "What a fool I am for lying in bed feeling sorry for myself when we still have two children to care for and one of them is sick."

She got up, dressed and tended to Lloyd. Edith and Leo took turns setting at Lloyd's bedside. Again they sent for the doctor and he promptly went to the ranch. It was only stomach flu but because of the loss of three sons, there was a great deal of worry. Relief came three days later when Lloyd wanted to go outside. They knew any possible danger had passed.

The winter of 1926-27 was terrible, more so west of Chadron and in eastern Wyoming. The temperature stayed below zero many days, and the snow fell over and over again. Several livestock herds were decimated. The Furman's had moved their cattle and horses to the south side of the river that fall. The bluff on the north side of the river and trees along the river gave some protection from the wind and snow. This also meant the animals would be closer to the house and barn.

Another precaution Leo took was to tie a rope from the house to the barn the day before Thanksgiving. He had learned this trick from his father. This safety guide would allow him to find his way back and forth on those days that the snow fell so fast and hard that you could not see more than two feet in front of your face.

Most of that winter they got hay to the cattle, but sometimes with great difficulty. Only twice was it so bad for a long period of time that they could not get out to check on or feed the livestock. When spring came they felt fortunate to have just lost 10 cows. However, that loss meant a loss of 10 calves also.

Spring brought new life to plants and animals. Edith felt the need to take part in bringing new life forth. She decided to do so by raising chicks. She began by gathering bushel baskets and boxes or anything else she could put a lid on. Then she would put dirt in the bottom of each. Next she put in straw. Old hens were placed on each nest and the lids kept the hens in place. In the meantime she saved the biggest eggs each day. Later when the hens were adjusted to setting, she placed the saved eggs under them. Three weeks later the little chicks began hatching out.

Anna Christensen was living with Edith and Leo. She was the teacher at the one-room school by the river. She invited Amy to go to school with her, even though Amy was not yet of school age. As it happened, that was the day that the county school superintendent came to the school to evaluate the school and the teacher. Not realizing Amy was not a pupil, she began to test Amy, since she was not responding like the other children were. Anna was not sure what to say, fearing she could be in trouble for allowing Amy to be there.

The superintendent felt she needed to show Anna how to teach by example. So she told Amy to go to the front of the room and get one book, then bring it to her. Amy did. Next she told Amy to bring her two books and count them. Amy did. This process was repeated another three times. After Amy handed her five books she said, "If you want any more books, get them yourself. You're fat and I don't like you." Amy sat down.

The surprised superintendent told Anna to go outside with her. Anna explained, "Amy is not a pupil. I had invited her to school because she lost a brother in February. I thought it might help both Amy and the family."

"You must first think of educating students, not doing welfare work. I will speak to the school board about this, but I feel you should be reprimanded." Anna was shocked. That evening Leo said, "Anna, as you know I am president of the school board here and you are going to be the teacher as long as you want to be. Forget about what you were told today. I appreciate what you were trying to do."

Anna taught for two more years; then she met a young man, got married and moved to Hay Springs.

In the summer James went out to help Jay and Leo stack hay. The conversation that day centered on buying land. James began by telling the boys about a half section of land for sale east of the ranch. "Pa, that half section is over five miles from us. That's too far to move cattle or hay. It's closer to the Jackson's than us. Tell them about it."

"I realize it's too far east for us, but if we owned it I think we could trade with John Tinnin for some of his land which is next to the south place."

"Why wouldn't he just buy it for himself? Then he wouldn't have to deal with us."

"I don't think the bank or anyone else will loan him the money to buy land. I also know he'd like to expand to the east. If we traded with him, he wouldn't have to borrow any money."

"Pa, I say forget it. We just about have all our loans paid off. Let's not start getting new ones."

"I already bought it."

"Where did you get the money?"

"I mortgaged a half section on the north place."

"Pa, how could you? You deeded two thirds of the north place to Leo and me."

"Well, I still own one third and that's what I mortgaged. Maybe I should have talked to you first, but I am doing it for your benefit."

"Not much we can do about it now. I just hope it'll work out."

"It will and I'll deed one third of it to you and one third to Leo."

A trade was worked out, but the Furman's had to include two teams of horses and a bull. When the price for cattle began to fall drastically and continue to slide for the next five years, it became a hardship to pay off the loan. No longer could they expect to receive $59 a head. Finally, in 1934, it bottomed out at $17.50 a head. At least they had calves to sell during those hard years, but income declined dramatically.

One good thing that happened during this time, Edith and Leo had another child. Evelyn was born on April 7, 1928. The morning she was born Leo sent the hired hand, Sam, after Evelyn Jackson. Herb and Evelyn Jackson were good friends of the Furman's and Evelyn was a midwife that had helped with many births in the area. "Sam, go over to the Jackson's and tell Mrs. Jackson to come over."

Sam told Evelyn, "Leo wants you to come over for a visit". Then he continued on to check on the fences on the north place. Sam didn't ask or know why Leo wanted Evelyn to visit. He just did what he was told. But the next morning when he went in for breakfast, there in his chair was a little baby girl, Evelyn Marie Furman. She was named after the good friend and midwife who delivered her. "Looks like I've been replaced by someone a lot prettier."

Edith and Leo wanted their children to enjoy life as children as they grew up. Still they wanted them to know work, so chores were assigned to them. The two carried firewood into the house. They fed chickens and gathered the eggs. And they were expected to work in the garden. But they were not to spend the majority of their time working like their parents had done as children. They also wanted them to have a complete education. As a result, Amy and Lloyd were playmates and got along very well together.

Amy had a dog named "Friday". He followed her everywhere. When she went to school he just lay around and waited for her to come home. He always seemed to know the time she got home. One day Friday died. Amy was heart broken. Later as Amy and Lloyd walked home from school she was thinking of Friday. "I wonder if Friday has gone to heaven." Lloyd piped up and said, "Not yet, he is still buried up there on that hill."

They had many stick horses which they lined up on the porch like real horses. Each one had a name. Of course, these horses had to be tamed before they were useful. Afterwards they were ridden many miles for many different reasons. As the two grew, they swam in the river and in a neighbor's pond. They were as innocent as Adam and Even in the Garden of Eden. It was not until Amy turned 10 that Edith told them they could no longer swim without some clothes on. Lloyd asked, "Why can't we swim naked?"

"Because Amy is becoming a young lady and ladies do not go around without their clothes."

In the winter they skated on the river with skates that clamped on their shoes. On cold days Edith made them put on so many coats, pants, and hats that they complained they could not move. But out the door they would run trying to see who would be the first on the frozen river.

Then in 1929 the world that everybody knew and enjoyed changed. Not only did the stock market crash, a significant business uncertainty began to develop. Banks failed and credit was not available to anyone. By the beginning of 1930 a sense of panic spread across the entire nation. City people lost their jobs. The problems spread into the farming and ranching communities. The ability to buy material things, or even food, began shrinking to a very few people. Farmers and ranchers found there was no longer a market for what they produced. No one had the money to buy anything. The sand hills region did remain financially intact; however, the people there struggled and suffered just like everyone else.

The three Furman families on the ranch met together. James said, "I've seen bad times before and your mother and I have always made it through them. We can all do so now, no matter how long this lasts."

"Pa's right. We've had an abundance of produce from the garden and we have meat and eggs. We're not going to starve."

"Yes, Jay, but this may last longer than a year."

Edith said she could make any clothes anyone needed. Leo said, "That just leaves the debt we owe the bank. Where are we going to get the cash for that?"

There was silence, then Jay commented, "Do you think Evan would loan us some money? He still seems to be doing alright."

"I am sure he would if he could, but he may need all the cash he has before this is over." Struggle they did to find cash, but they always came up with enough to at least pay the interest on the due dates.

No one realized that it would be almost a decade before it would be completely over. During the 1930's there would be periods of betterment and then recession would set in again.

Little things brought joy and relief, such as ice cream. In the winter, snow and ice from the river could be used for ice cream making. In the summer ice cream could still be made as long as the ice held out in the ice house. Amy and Lloyd took turns cranking the paddles in the ice cream freezer. Their reward was licking the paddles as soon as the ice cream hardened.

Jay and his daughter, Helen, would go to visit Leo, Edith and their children quite often. Evelyn was always happy when they came. Jay always paid a lot of attention to her and would make funny noises and sounds. Evelyn's favorite was his honking like a goose. She soon began referring to Jay as Uncle Goose.

Amy and Lloyd both were animal lovers. Amy wanted to make every new calf born near the barn a pet. Lloyd seemed to sense the cows were the family's livelihood and must be protected and nurtured.

Lloyd was only eight years old the first time he was allowed to take part in moving cattle to better grass. Leo watched him very closely and never put him into any situation where he could be hurt. Yet Leo smiled to himself as he watched Lloyd. He said out loud, but no one heard, "The place will be in good hands when Lloyd takes over some day."

CHAPTER 9
A TIME TO TEAR DOWN AND A TIME TO BUILD

In the spring of 1930, James, still obsessed with owning land, bought a half section west of the north place from Walter Wamsley. Walter needed money to pay his debts and James believed he could buy the land for a very reasonable price. They finally agreed to a price of $21,600. James had the $600 but he had to borrow $21,000. Jay and Leo were not pleased with the purchase and let James know it. "You boys will be glad I bought it someday wait and see. I could just transfer it to both of you now."

"Yes, and we'll have the mortgage to pay, too."

The spring came with almost no rainfall. That summer it was worse. Jay and Leo cut grass for winter hay every place they could find. There would be no surplus and if the winter was long, they would be in trouble.

The winter of 1930 did not have much snowfall; cold but little snow. That seemed like a good thing at the time. Unfortunately it was the beginning of a long-term drought. Normal rainfall would not return to the sand hills until the spring of 1940. The spring of 1931 brought new calves and no birth problems for a change. What it didn't bring was rain. The summer came and left without rain.

"We don't have enough hay to make it through another winter."

"I know, Leo. Any suggestions?"

James answered first, "We don't have any choice. When we sell the steers this fall we'll have to sell some of the cows, too."

"Pa, that means fewer calves for at least two to three years."

"Yes, but if we don't sell some of the cows they'll starve to death. All the other ranchers are faced with the same problem, so no one is going to have any hay to sell."

"Jay, how many do you think we could feed through the winter?"

"I don't know, Leo. It'll depend on how much rainfall we get. You know that."

"Boys, I think we should sell at least 75 cows, maybe 100."

When the steers went to market, 100 cows went also. But lack of hay was not the only problem. The garden did not provide the usual supply of vegetables because of the lack of rainfall. Edith had carried water and tried to coax as much as possible from the soil. The only thing it got her was a sore leg that kept her from walking for three days. What had happened was her trick knee went out of joint and she fell in the garden and could not get up. She had a knee injury from falling out of a wagon when she was a child. When she fell, she called her two dogs to her, placed her hands on their backs and pushed herself up. Using them as a crutch and her one good leg, she struggled back to the house. Amy and Lloyd saw her struggling and helped her onto the porch. "Mama, what happened? Are you alright?"

"Yes, it's just my knee went out on me."

"Sit down, I'll go get Papa." Then Amy put a bridle on Sparky and rode off to find her father. Leo returned with Amy. He wanted to go on to town for the doctor. Edith said, "Don't make such a fuss. I'll be alright."

"Well, you just sit for a day or two. The kids and I will take care of the house and garden."

About half of the normal amount of food was canned and dried for the winter. Even egg production was down from normal. The choke-cherries and June berries were very scarce that year so there was little jelly made; a big disappointment to the Furman men. Only meat was available in normal quantities. A lot of beef and chicken was eaten that winter. Canned vegetables almost became a luxury.

Mortgage payments were starting to fall behind. The three Furman men went into the bank to ask for more time in making payment. The only concession obtained was that they could pay just the interest and let the principle stay the same. They went to the land bank and borrowed the money to pay the interest on the Rushville bank loan.

When they returned to the ranch, Leo said to Edith, "This ranch cannot support three families. Since I'm the youngest, I should be the one to leave. Do you think we could survive someplace else?"

"If that's how you feel, we should go. Maybe you could work for some of the neighbors."

"I'll find someone who could use me and provide us with a place to live. Tomorrow we'll tell Ma and Pa we plan to leave as soon as I find some work."

Leo and Edith walked into the kitchen of the stone house early the next morning. James and Belle were still eating breakfast and Jay was in the barn milking. "You folks are up early. Want some coffee?"

"Sure. Edith and I have something to tell you."

"We can guess that. Is there a problem?"

"The problem is three families cannot make a living on this ranch with things being the way they are, so Edith and I are going to move as soon as I find work someplace."

Belle was surprised, "Leo, you've lived your whole life on this ranch. How could you think of moving?"

"It's not easy, Ma. But I think our going will make it better for you and Pa, and Jay, too. And I know I can get work on another place."

"Leo, please stay. Your father is too old to work all day anymore and Jay cannot run the place by himself. You probably could, but not Jay. If you go, things will only get worse and we'll never pay off our debts."

"I don't know Ma. Guess I never stopped to think about Pa getting so old. But I don't see how three families can stay here."

"Well, three families have been making it for the last three years and nobody has starved. I want you to stay as well as your mother does."

Edith had been quiet, but now put her hand on Leo's arm and said, "Maybe we should think about it some more, Leo."

"Son, families stick together in bad times as well as good times. It isn't going to be any better for any of us if you and Edith leave the place."

"Like Edith says, we'll think about it some more. I guess there's no hurry to do anything." They decided to stay.

Evan had been reasonably successful in the automobile business in Gordon. One day he had found a young bulldog that he felt sorry for and took it to his garage in Gordon. When Leo was in Gordon, he stopped in to visit with Evan. The dog took a shine to Leo instantly, so Evan asked Leo if he would like to have the dog. "You know I like dogs. I'll take him home to the kids."

All three were thrilled to have a new dog, especially Evelyn. They named him Spike. Since Amy and Lloyd were in school, Spike became Evelyn's playmate. Spike did whatever Evelyn wanted him to do. She would put him on a chair and dress him in any clothes she could find. Once she found a pair of bright red ladies silk bloomers that Edith was going to put into a rug she was hooking. After some effort Evelyn got the bloomers on Spike. By that time Spike had had enough, he jumped off the chair and ran out the door. He did not stop until he was a good 50 yards away. Edith happened to look out the window and saw this red object flittering around. She couldn't figure out what it was. Out she went to investigate. There was Spike in what was going to be a rag rug. "Evelyn, what have you been doing to that poor dog? You can just sit in the corner the rest of the afternoon."

Sometimes when Edith went to town, Evelyn would fall asleep in the back seat of the car. Spike liked to ride in the front seat with his head out the window. Rather than wake Evelyn, Edith just left her in the car with Spike while she traded eggs, butter and cream for flour and sugar. But as soon as Edith left, Spike jumped into the back seat and stood guard over Evelyn.

1933 brought back the sales of beer and whiskey. Jay was the first to notice. "Leo, the saloon in town is back in business. You can get a drink legally now. Want to go get one?"

"No, thanks. Money is too scarce and too valuable to spend it on whiskey."

"That's true, but I wouldn't mind having a little whiskey."

The entire family was involved in any possible way to make money. Edith, Amy and Lloyd would hitch a team of horses to a wagon and drive along the river bed looking for old animal bones. Old bones were purchased by companies that made fertilizer. A wagon load of bones could be sold for $7.00. Even little Evelyn would go on these hunts. She was thrilled when she found a bone.

Finally the rains came in 1934. They had been praying for rain for three years. So much rain answered their prayers that the Niobrara River flooded. The bridge connecting the ranch washed out. It broke apart as it washed down stream. Not only did this handicap the Furman's, it also hurt many neighbors to the south because this was the main way to Rushville. If it was necessary to go to Rushville, those folks now had to go east to the Gordon road, then north to the town of Gordon, then west to Rushville. Usually they stopped in Gordon and bought from those merchants, which made the Rushville merchants unhappy.

Leo and Edith took their automobile this long way around and just left it on the north side of the river. Whenever they needed to go to town, they took off their shoes and waded across the river. Amy and Lloyd didn't mind at all, but Edith didn't like it at all since she had to hold her dress up to wade the river. Once she slipped and got her dress too wet to go on to town. After that she only left the ranch when it was absolutely necessary.

Everyone wanted the bridge replaced. Unfortunately there was no money available. Neither the county nor individuals could pay for a new bridge. Finally a low wooden bridge was built across the river. This lasted until another flood came a few years later.

Jay's daughter, Helen Isabelle, had graduated and continued on at school to get her teaching license. A teaching license could be obtained after completing one additional year of study. Now that she was grown, Jay missed having a female in his life. He had not paid much attention to the lady teaching in the one-room school by the river. As if some revelation had suddenly hit him, he seemed to suddenly realize not only was she single, she was also pretty.

When school was over that spring, Jay married Mary Ofzarzak. They lived with James and Belle in the stone house. This arrangement lasted one year. Jay and his wife moved to Martin, South Dakota. One other factor that contributed to the move was sheep. Mary's family had always raised sheep and she convinced Jay he should try raising sheep. James and Leo had always been cattlemen. They were not as receptive to the idea of raising sheep as Jay was. There was coexistence for awhile, but it became obvious there was a strain on relationships.

"Leo, I know you and Pa are not too pleased with raising sheep, but I see some benefit to having sheep as well as cattle. If you'll help me get a stake someplace else, I'll sign my third of the ranch over to you."

Leo was stunned! "Are you sure you want to do that?"

"Yes, I've thought about it for a month now and Mary agrees with me. We want to be on our own."

"OK. I'll have to borrow some money. How much do you want?"

"We only need enough to buy a section or so and I'd like to have some of the cattle."

"When you find a place, let me know what it might cost. One third of the cattle belong to you already, so you should take them. We can move them with some help. Have you told Pa?"

"No, I wanted to talk to you first."

Jay had not looked long when he found out about some land available west of Martin, South Dakota. After checking it out, he discovered he could also lease some Indian land next to the land for sale. An agreed price of $50 an acre was reached. Leo would need to borrow $3,200. Edith felt they were so far in debt that they would never survive.

That summer, Jay, Leo, Amy, Lloyd and the hired man by the name of Ralph Taylor moved livestock into Rushville and loaded them on the train for a trip to Merriman. It was a distance of 45 miles with another 25 miles north to Jay's new place. They drove the cattle and sheep up the road to Martin and then on to Jay's place. Lloyd and Amy took turns riding point. Leo and Jay took turns trailing while Ralph rode the left side. When Jay and his wife left, James and Belle's widowed daughter, Mary, moved in with them to take care of Belle. Mary had been teaching school, but felt the need to help her parents.

1935 was another year of no rain. One August day when Leo was riding in a wagon pulled by Prince and Maud, he stopped to replace a broken fence post. He looked west and saw this huge, dark cloud coming toward him. It not only covered the entire sky, it was all the way down to the ground. Leo knew it could only be one thing – a dust storm. He had seen a small one previously, but nothing like what he saw at the moment. He left the wagon and tools, climbed on Prince and grabbed Maud's reigns and headed for the barn. He made it to the river, but not the barn. Leo could not see beyond the ears on Prince. He urged the horses across the river and pointed them in the direction of what he thought would be the barn. He let Prince find the way, which he did. Leo got both horses inside and closed the door. There was nothing more he could do but wait out the storm. He hoped Edith and the kids were in the house.

Two hours later the wind died down. Leo had never seen so much sand in the barn. He would have to shovel it out. That could wait. He hurried to the house. The front door had sand piled against it so he went to the back door. It was clear. Edith had already started sweeping up sand that had blown in around the doors and windows. The sand had even blown down the stovepipe and was in the cooking stove. "Where are Amy and Lloyd?"

"They are in their bedrooms sweeping up sand. It's everywhere. There's even sand in the potato bin!" It took two days to clean all the sand out of the house, barn, and tool shed.

Mary, James and Belle's youngest daughter, married again to Ralph Taylor in October. She had been widowed for 12 years. They lived with James and Belle that winter. In December James turned 77 and he developed pneumonia. Mary and Belle did what they could. On the morning of January 18, 1936 Belle took a tray of food to James and found him in a talkative mood. "Belle, I remember one Sunday morning the preacher talked about God being the owner of the entire world. I used to always think in terms of how you and I built this place and a herd of cattle. Now I realize it was God that allowed us to do that. We just got to own the land for a little while."

"James, it sounds like you finally got to know the Lord personally."

"I have; and something else. I want you to know that I always loved you and appreciated everything you have done."

"It is nice to hear you say that. I love you, too. Now eat something; I'll come back later."

When Belle went back to get the tray, James was dead.

The morning James died, Ralph went to get Leo and Edith. They all returned and Ralph went on into Rushville to call Evan, Jay and their sisters. It was a week before the entire family could come together. The funeral home kept James' body outside so it would not decompose. The grave had to be dug with pickaxes because of the frozen ground. The man who had lived 50 of his 77 years in the sand hills and thought so much of the land was now a part of it.

Part of James' obituary read:

> *He was always an advocate of the importance of good schooling; he attended school obtaining a teachers' certificate and taught school in Iowa. He was baptized into the Methodist Episcopal Church. In 1887 he brought his family and a carload of personal property to his homestead 14 miles southeast of Rushville. This homestead became the nucleus of the present Furman ranch, which was acquired piece by piece at the cost of great personal sacrifice and effort through the very trying years.*

After the funeral the family went to the stone house to mourn and reminisce.

They talked about how positive their father had been until the automobile sales business broke him. Jay said, "He loved the ranch and he never seemed to think he owned enough land."

Leona commented, "Well, I remember his temper." The boys talked about their memories of their father.

Mary listened for awhile and then said, "I remember a poem someone wrote. I don't know who, but it is going through my mind just now.

> *'Nothing but memories as we journey on,*
> *Longing for a smile from someone gone.*
> *Thoughts return to scenes now past.*
> *Time rolls on, but memories last.'*

"Leo, you're the only one left on the ranch. It's up to you to take care of the place and look after Ma."

"I know, Evan. Edith and I'll make sure Ma's alright." The ranch was now in Belle and Leo's names and so were the mortgages.

Amy and Lloyd completed the eighth grade at the school by the river that spring. After school was out, Lyle Jackson dropped by to convince Leo they should go to the International Livestock Show in Chicago. Lyle Jackson was a brother to Evan's first wife, Milla. The Jackson's and the Furman's were close friends. Both families had ranches and raised Black Angus cattle.

"Lyle, Chicago's a long way from here. I'd like to go, but money is very tight right now."

"Leo, it won't cost as much as you think and besides we need to meet people who buy cattle and raise bulls. Where would be a better place to do that?"

"Let me think it over."

"OK. I plan to go and take the family. You should consider doing the same."

That night Leo talked to Edith. "Lyle and his family are going to Chicago to a livestock show and they want us to go with them. I'd like to do it, but the cost scares me."

"Leo, I'm sure we could find the money someplace. Let's go. It would be great for the children."

Plans were made and train tickets were purchased. Amy, Lloyd and Evelyn were excited about the trip. Chicago was overwhelming to them and they were ready to return home by the third day. They were homesick. Lloyd had taken his harmonica along and he often played "Home Sweet Home", which didn't cheer his sisters up at all.

When they finally got back to the ranch, Amy did not feel good. "Amy, you need a hot bath and a good night's sleep. You'll feel better in the morning."

While Amy was taking her bath, Edith picked up Evelyn to put her in bed only to have her faint in her arms. "Leo, help me! Something's wrong with the children." Leo took Evelyn and Edith went back to check on Amy. As Amy was drying off, Edith saw the problem – measles. The next morning Lloyd had them, too.

"Edith, the kids being sick is a result of our trip. This is what happens when you're in big cities and around a lot of people. We should've never gone."

"Now, Leo, you don't know that. They could have gotten the measles in Rushville just as easy."

"Oh, no, the Indians never had all these diseases until the white man introduced them. Out here people are not as apt to get so many diseases."

"I'll agree the more people there are, the bigger the chance of catching something. But we can't just become hermits."

"Well, I am just happy that we don't live in a big city!"

During the summer the school superintendent and Rushville High School principal made a visit to the ranch. They informed Leo in no uncertain terms that he was to send Amy and Leo to town to attend high school in the fall. Their forceful conversation did not set well with Leo.

"Don't tell me what my children have to do or where they have to go. I will make those decisions. If you want to come back and just visit fine, but don't ever tell me that I have to turn my children over to the two of you."

After overhearing the conversation, Edith asked that night, "Now how can the children finish their education? You and your bull-headedness are going to cause a big problem some day."

"Maybe so, I just don't like being told I have to do something. As for Amy and Lloyd going to high school, they can take courses through the mail from the state." They took the correspondence courses for three years under the supervision of Mrs. Bratherson.

Evelyn continued going to the one room school with one other student who was older than she. His name was Robert Riggs. In the fall of 1938 Robert entered high school in Rushville. That left Evelyn the only student in the little school. So the school closed. Edith convinced Leo that the children needed to go to town to school.

Amy, Lloyd, and Evelyn drove to Rushville every day that school term. When snowstorms came they did not go, or they stayed in town with friends if the snowstorms happened while they were it school. After graduation Amy continued to take post-graduate work at the high school so she could teach school. This provided transportation for Evelyn for another year. After that she boarded in town with the Sipp family during the school sessions.

On a late October day in 1937 Jay went to talk to Leo about buying one or two bulls from his upcoming spring calves. The two brothers had a great visit and Leo said he would save two prosperous looking males in the spring. Jay stopped at his mother's house on his return trip. Belle cooked supper and suggested he spend the night. Jay was more than agreeable to the suggestion since it was late when they finished talking.

The next morning when Jay left, Belle walked out with him to his car. The front step was icy from the frost. Belle's feet slid out from under her and she fell hard. "Mom, are you alright?" Her left leg was turn to one side.

"My leg hurts something fearful. Help me up. Yeow! That hurts too much."

"Mom, I'll carry you inside. Your leg may be broken." Jay carried Belle into her bedroom. He brought her a pitcher of water and said, "I'm going to town for the doctor and I'll be back as soon as I can. Try not to move while I'm gone." He drove as fast as possible to the main road and then raced into Rushville. The doctor was just opening his office when Jay drove up. "Doctor, I think my mother broke her leg and she's alone right now. Can you go out to her?"

"I don't seem to have any patients at the moment so I'll get some splinting material and go with you." Jay returned at a somewhat slower rate. After the doctor examined Belle, he said, "You didn't break your leg, you broke your hip. I'll realign it the best I can and then wrap it. But you're not going to be able to walk for some time. You'll need someone to take care of you until you can move around on your own."

Jay asked the doctor to stay with Belle while he drove to Leo's house. Edith went back with Jay. "Jay, I can stay with Belle some, but not all day every day. Ask Milla DeWitt if she could come out and stay some. I know she has a new baby, but she could bring the baby and her daughter, too."

"I'll go by her house and ask after I take the doctor back to town."

Milla was Evan's youngest daughter and a niece of Leo and Edith. Her husband delivered gasoline to Leo and all the other farmers and ranchers in the area. Milla was willing to help, and agreed to stay as much as she could. She would ask Larry, her husband, to take her out to Belle's house in the morning.

The next morning Milla, her daughter, Kathleen, and her fussy newborn son arrived in time to help prepare lunch for Belle. Edith, Milla and Belle exchanged all the news in the area. Milla kept trying to nurse her son, Lawrence, without any success. Milla had tried everything she could think of, but Lawrence would not nurse.

Belle said, "Bring him to me and bring me a saucer of cream." Belle put her finger in the cream, then into Lawrence's mouth. Nothing happened, so Belle repeated the process. This time Lawrence smacked his lips. Soon he was taking to the finger sucking.

In a week he was taking a bottle and putting on weight. Belle always seemed to know what to do. In this case she saved Lawrence's life.

With help from Edith, Amy and Milla, Belle recovered to the point where she could manage by herself. "You three go home and take care of your families and quit fussing over me. I can take care of myself."

Edith said, "Belle, why don't you come and live with Leo and me."

"I'm fine and want to live in my own home."

Edith could not persuade Belle to leave, so both women left for their own homes.

1937 and 1938 were rebuilding years. Leo, with a great deal of help, moved the little house near the stone house south across the river and put it across the garden from Edith and his house. This was for the hired man and his family. The old barn became a calving shed and a new bigger barn was built. This barn had stanchions for the cows that were milked and there were five stalls for horses. One was a large box stall. The loft was above the horse stalls. There was a track and pulley across the peak of the roof that accommodated a sling arrangement to pull hay up and into the loft before it was dumped. This was done with horses. The new barn was painted red. Amy suggested, "We should put our name on the front of the barn above the loft door."

Lloyd added, "Yes, and our brand, too." So over the door to the loft was painted a large ⌒**F**⌒ and **FURMAN**.

The house they had lived in for 24 years, which James and Belle had lived in before, was torn down. A new house was built. There was a windmill with a high reservoir beside the new house, which provided water to the house and a horse tank. Some of the water went through a heavy box that Leo had built to keep milk and butter cool in the summer. One day when Evelyn went to get butter for her mother, a kitten went along. Evelyn raised the lid and the kitten just had to see what was inside the box. It perched on the edge of the box. The heavy lid fell down too fast for the kitten to jump down. The kitten's death upset Evelyn for days. Lloyd was mad at her because he had to clean up the mess and bury the kitten.

Men were hired to build the new house. At the same time other hired men were working to put up hay for the winter. Edith had her hands full cooking for so many men. Amy helped until she was recruited to drive the raking team in the hay field. Little Evelyn tried to replace Amy in the kitchen.

Amy was doing fine until a bumblebee stung old Ned. Ned and Maud ran away. Amy was yelling, "Whoa! Whoa!" She could not get them stopped. Her efforts caused her to fall off the seat onto the rake frame. She was hanging on by one caught leg when Leo saw what was happening. He jumped from the haystack he was on and mounted a horse that was tied nearby. He raced across the field after the runaway team, stopping them. Amy could have been killed if she had fallen under the rake. "Amy, are you alright? What happened?"

"I must have driven over a bumblebee nest because a bee stung Ned. My leg hurts, but I guess I am alright."

"You go back to the house and ask your Ma to look you over." Leo put Amy on the horse and sent her to the house. He took the team back to where they were stacking hay.

A few weeks after they had finished cutting and stacking hay, Leo told Lloyd, "I want you to check the fences north of the river. Try to count how many cows and how many calves are there. The last time I went to town I noticed the grass bent over where a vehicle had driven."

"Dad, do you think someone stole some cattle?"

"I don't know. If they did, it won't be the first time. Not much we can do about it either, unless we catch them."

"I hope none of the cattle are missing. I'll try to get a good count. We repaired all the bad places in the fences last spring so they should be in good shape. I'll start out first thing tomorrow morning."

The next morning Lloyd left on his horse, taking water and a lunch with him. The morning was uneventful. Then early in the afternoon he found a broken fencepost and the barbwires on the ground. Since he didn't have a replacement post or any tools, Lloyd tried to prop up the post and reattach the wires. While he was doing so, he heard a calf bawling. The noise was coming from near the river. He mounted his horse and headed toward the sound. He soon saw four cows and three calves. The fourth calf was in the river's edge, but stuck. Even though the water was only five or six inches deep, the calf's legs had sunk into soft sand until its belly was almost touching the water. The calf could not move.

Lloyd tied a rope around the calf's body right behind its front legs, and then wrapped the other end of the rope around the saddle horn. He mounted and encouraged the horse forward. The calf cried out in its loudest voice while its mother joined in with loud moos. The horse drug the calf out of the river and away from the water. The calf did not seem to be injured, but Lloyd had to wrestle it in order to untie the rope around it. Then he had to herd all eight animals back to where they had gotten out. Getting them back on the other side of the fence was no easy matter for just one man and one horse. After a great deal of yelling and a little cussing, he succeeded.

Lloyd finished what he could in making temporary fence repairs and started back to the barn to get a new post, tools and staples to fix the post properly. He returned to the broken fence in the pickup and made the repairs. By this time it was beginning to get dark. Tomorrow would be another day and he would start all over again.

Lloyd

The wooden bridge which had washed out twice in the last few years was finally replaced by a high steel bridge by the state. This bridge had been located on a state highway. The state built and paved a new road south from Rushville. This was about five miles west of the ranch. Where it crossed the river a new bridge was built. The old one was cut into three sections and one section was moved down stream to replace the wooden bridge over the river on the Furman ranch.

After the new house was built, Belle went to live with Leo and Edith because she could no longer live alone. She had trouble walking and only left her bedroom to eat meals. On January 17, 1939 Belle died, one day short of three years after James' death. The family gathered together again.

After the funeral, the conversation turned to what was going to be the disposal of the ranch. Would it be divided up among them? It didn't take long for Evan to wade in. "Leo has stayed on the ranch and kept it going. We all left. He has taken care of our mother and father, too, for that matter. The ranch should be his alone and if anybody tries to make it otherwise, I'll shoot them." That ended the discussion.

It was quiet for several minutes, then Jay said, "Don't get all worked up, Evan. We realize Leo has kept the ranch going, and he should get a bigger share."

"Leo gets it all. I meant what I said."

There was no more discussion.

Chapter 10
A Time for War

That first Christmas in the new house Evelyn convinced her mother and father that they should have a Christmas tree. "Mother, one day at school Bud and Shirley Dewing told me they put a pine tree in their house at Christmas time. They string popcorn to put on it and even place candles on some of the branches. Can we do that?"

"If it is alright with your father, it is alright with me." Evelyn went looking for her father.

"Can we have a pine tree in the house and decorate it for Christmas like the Dewing's do?"

"What in the world does a pine tree have to do with the birth of Christ?"

"Nothing really, Papa. It just makes a home more festive and bright. And it also gives a house a fresh pine smell. I read about it in a magazine."

"I guess there's nothing wrong with that. What does your mother say?"

"She said to ask you."

"Must be alright with her then. You ask Lloyd if he'll cut a pine tree for you and set it up in the house. Then you and Amy can decorate it. Are you going to hang your stocking on it?"

"I don't know. I'll ask Amy."

Lloyd and Amy were too old for stockings, but they continued to hang them for Evelyn's sake. That Christmas the stockings were pinned to the back of a chair like always. On Christmas morning each stocking contained an orange and some candy. Evelyn's also contained a rag doll that Edith had made.

Evelyn was at the age where she thought chores were never ending. And there really was always work to do, like keeping the wood box full. Even in the summer some wood would be needed for the cooking stove. The children were responsible for carrying in wood and making sure the box was always full when they got home from school. When Evelyn was younger she carried only a few sticks. Now she was 11, she carried more and in another two years the wood would be piled high on her arms. Lloyd and Amy did most of the milking and Evelyn would help feed the milk cows or just simply watch.

Lloyd called Evelyn over to where he was milking. "Evelyn, it's time you learn to milk. Come here. Now sit close to the cow's hind leg, lean into her a little bit, that way she can't raise her leg and kick the bucket. You need to be all the way under her. Put the bucket between your legs and hold it with your legs. Now bend your thumbs into the palm of your hand and put your fingers around two teats and squeeze and pull down."

"Like this?"

"That's it. When you can't get any more milk, do the same to the other two teats. Oh, one other thing – don't milk them too dry or their quarters will stick together."

"Evelyn, don't pay any attention to that last part. Lloyd is just spoofing you about their quarters sticking together. You did fine. I'll just finish stripping her."

In 1939 Leo purchased a wind charger to generate electricity and batteries to store the charge. The whole family was excited. No more lanterns to be cleaned and no more mantles to fuss about. No more kerosene smell in the house. There was a light bulb in every room and now there was even a radio in the living room! Everyone gathered around the radio after the evening chores were finished and supper dishes were washed. Leo always wanted to hear Lowell Thomas reporting the evening news. The family especially enjoyed listening to Amos and Andy.

That summer Margaret Fisher, who was Lloyd's girlfriend, wanted to borrow his horse, Ned. Ned was a beautiful, shiny black horse with one white foreleg. He was a very impressive, spirited horse. Margaret had been chosen to be the Queen of the Sheridan County Fair and Rodeo. She wanted to ride Ned in the Main Street Parade for the opening of the fair and rodeo. This was Ned's first trip to Rushville. The crowd, the cars, and the noise excited him. He was quite a sight prancing down the street with his ears up. Lloyd thought Margaret sitting on Ned was the most beautiful sight he had ever seen. He was spending more and more time with Margaret.

On a clear day in May, Leo rode up to the barn with a rope around the neck of a new colt. Lloyd was replacing boards on a hay wagon and Evelyn was helping; or so she thought. She had been asking Lloyd all kinds of questions while he was working.

"What or who have you got, Pa?"

"Topsy's colt. She had a badly broken leg and I had to shoot her. It looked like she'd been running and stepped into a prairie dog hole and fell."

"I hate to hear that, she was a good horse. So what do we do with the colt?"

"We'll have to bottle feed her until she can fend for herself. Evelyn, I want you to be responsible for feeding this colt. Amy can show you how to bottle feed her."

"I'd like that, Pa."

"I'll leave her in the corral for now."

The colt became a pet. She had the freedom of the barnyard and the yard around the house. She even made her way into the garden where her favorite snack was the tops of onions. Whenever she was hungry, she would try to nuzzle Evelyn. Evelyn would push her away because she reeked of onions. "Get away! Your breath is terrible." The colts name soon became Onions. Onions became a nuisance that was tolerated until she became too large to wander around the yard.

Amy completed her requirements to get a teacher's license. In the fall of 1940 she began teaching in a one-room school not far from the ranch. She continued to live with Leo and Edith for the next six years while she taught school; most of the time she rode Ned back and forth to the schoolhouse.

In the spring of 1940 the rains returned to normal and the financial condition improved. There was a good price for steers that fall. Leo was able to reduce the debt on the ranch.

In early November of 1941 Leo and Edith went to a bull sale in Alliance. Lloyd and Margaret went with them. While Leo and Edith were looking over bulls and talking with Lyle and Margaret Jackson, Lloyd and Margaret slipped away and got married. When it was time to go home, Lloyd and Margaret were missing. No one had seen them all afternoon. Edith wanted to search for them, but Leo said, "They're grown adults. Let them find a way to get home. Besides they probably left with some friends. Let's go home; I have evening chores to do."

The next day Lloyd and Margaret showed up in a rented buggy. They both had a very sheepish look on their faces. Leo was out in the barn and Edith was sewing. She just gave them the – you better explain – look. "Ma, we got married yesterday."

"What? I don't know what to say. Why did you sneak off to get married?"

"We didn't exactly sneak off, Ma. We've been thinking about it for a long time and, well, when we were in Alliance we just thought, why not now? So we went over to the Presbyterian Church and got the preacher to marry us."

Leo walked up just in time to hear the last of the conversation. "Son, you're old enough to marry, but your Mother and I would have liked to have been there. I wish you would have told us ahead of time."

"I'm sorry. I guess we were just thinking of ourselves."

"Well, it's done now. So have you thought about where you are going to live?"

"There's no one living in the little house. Could we live there?"

"That's fine. I guess two rooms are enough when you are young and in love. But you'll have to clean it up. And it'll be up to you to keep it up."

On December 7, 1941 Japan attacked Pearl Harbor. War would bring changes to the entire nation. Food, clothing, gasoline and most everything was rationed. Prices on everything started to climb. Quickly the government put a ceiling on prices. Beef was in demand, not only by people, but also by the military. Leo found he could sell all the steers he had at a good price.

Soon young men began joining the military services. A neighbor, Ed Stamper, was one of the first to go. Ed had worked for Leo since he was 16 years old. Bud Dewing, a cousin, joined the Navy; Jay Furman's stories had influenced him. Several boys went as soon as school was over in the spring. The following summer Bob Shively, who had worked for Leo for several years, said to him one evening, "I was in town today and was told that Bill Sweeney was going to see to it that me and Lloyd were both drafted. He thinks that since you didn't go service in World War I like he and his brothers did, you were going to do pay up this time. Can he do that?"

"Well, he is on the draft board, but I don't think he can just send off those he doesn't like. There are rules he must follow."

"I don't know, Leo. I do know my wife and daughter can't make it on their own. My in-laws live in California and if I have to go she would need to stay with them. I talked things over with her and we both think we should move there to be closer to her parents in case I do get drafted."

"Bob, I can't promise you what is going to happen, but I will see to it that your wife and daughter get to California if you have to go."

"I figured you'd say that and I appreciate it. You've always been very fair with me. But I think it is best if we go now." Bob and his family left for California three days later.

That same summer Lloyd built a bedroom onto their house. Margaret was pregnant and two rooms were not going to be enough. In September, Rodney was born. Leo and Edith were as thrilled as Lloyd was. Their first grandchild would become very special to them.

Leo hired another man; his name was Boots Wilson. Boots was single and a good worker. Before a year was over Boots was drafted. Leo began to wonder if there was anything to what Bob Shively had told him. Leo still needed help and he found it in Cy Iron Cloud, a Sioux Indian. Cy became a friend of the family, as well as a good worker.

Iron Cloud & Edith

In 1942 the school principal went out to visit Leo and Edith. This visit was made by a different man and for a different reason. "Evelyn is a very exceptional pupil. She has great potential. We enjoy having her in our school. But I suggest you consider sending her to a different school so she can get a better education."

"Leo and I know Evelyn is smart, but we never thought about her going anyplace but here for school."

"That's fine. I would love to have her continue with us, but for her sake consider sending her to Jane Ivinson Memorial Hall in Laramie, Wyoming. It is an Episcopalian School for girls and it is connected to the University of Wyoming. She'll get an education beyond high school level."

"Her mother and I'll talk to her and see if she'd like to go there." Evelyn not only went that fall, she would graduate with honors and received an all expense paid scholarship to the University of Wyoming. Her time at home was limited for the next four years.

When she left the first time, Edith told Leo, "I want us to get a telephone. The line is out to the Kearn's place. Let's see if it can be extended on out to us."

"I think it could be if we paid for it."

"Well, whatever it cost I'd like to see it done so Evelyn can call us if she needs something. Besides I want to be able to talk to her once in a while." Before winter set in, there was a new telephone in the main house.

During this time the war continued. The demand for beef meant a good income for the Furman's. With very little to purchase, money was going into savings and war bonds. The family's financial security improved tremendously. The mortgage was totally paid. For the first time since 1890 there was no mortgage on the ranch, which now consisted of 7,560 acres.

Leo and Lloyd as well as the hired help were kept extremely busy. Not only the normal work of raising cattle kept them occupied, but also the repairing of equipment and tools was a big workload. Replacement equipment could not be purchased any place. By necessity both

Leo and Lloyd became good at welding. Making do with what was available became a way of life.

On August 1, 1944 a draft notice came for Lloyd. Leo immediately went into Rushville to talk to the draft board members about a deferment for Lloyd. Board member Bill Sweeney said, "I'm not surprised to see you and I know why you are here. I'll tell you right now the answer is no."

"Bill, I don't know why you have it in for me and my family. But you have got to be fair. You know Lloyd is needed where he is. He's working to feed the military. Others have gotten a deferment to work farms and ranches. A deferment for Lloyd could be given as well."

"Maybe so, but your family is going to serve this time. You won't get off like you did in the First World War while my brothers and I were serving."

"My brother served in the navy then and the only reason I didn't serve was because I had scarlet fever which I didn't get over for a year. And I also have a bad leg. I was declared physically unfit for service."

"Don't expect any sympathy from me. Your boy is going."

Lloyd was to report for basic training on September 16, 1944. He left Margaret and Rodney at the train station. Leo and Edith said their goodbyes at the ranch. On the train to California Lloyd met Van from Ogalala, Nebraska. He also was to report for basic training. Lloyd and Van became good friends and completed training together. They never saw one another after basic training. Furloughs were granted after basic and Lloyd gladly went home. The time at home was all too short and Lloyd reported back to the port for shipment to Hawaii.

Edith's worry and nerves overcame her and she was very sick after Lloyd left. She had bad dreams night after night. Leo was concerned but did not know what to do. Evan's wife, Mary, came and stayed for a week and that seemed to help Edith.

At a Saturday night dance, Amy met Henry Rath. Henry had worked for some of the ranchers around Rushville. They began dating and were married May 6, 1945. The newlyweds rented a small house on land owned by Ike Jackson. It was not far from the Furman ranch. Hank, as Amy called him, continued working for Chris Abbot, a nearby rancher.

From Hawaii, Lloyd shipped out as a member of the 77th Infantry Division. They arrived at Okinawa early May, 1945. The fighting there had been going on for three weeks. A new friend was made by the name of Ray Hayes. Ray was from Texas and his family raised cattle also. The two talked a lot about raising cattle and the differences between Nebraska and Texas.

At first Lloyd's squad gave support to other units as they moved forward or brought their wounded back for treatment. Then on May 21st their group was ordered to make an attack on Sugar Loaf Hill. It was to be a night attack beginning at 3 o'clock in the morning. About halfway up the hill the 96th Division mistakenly opened fire on them. Lloyd's platoon had two men killed and six wounded before the mistake was corrected.

Then they continued on toward their objective. They soon discovered they either had to cross a wide open field and be exposed to enemy fire or follow a pass to start up the hill. The decision was made to go through the pass.

Too late they found it had been booby-trapped. Lloyd was on point, leading the others through when he stepped on a mine. He was killed instantly and two others were seriously wounded. Lloyd was the first of several buddies that Ray would lose. The war ended in August and Lloyd would have been 23 in September. He had been a quiet man who liked to raise horses. He had a talent for drawing horses and other things as well. Edith always thought he could have been an artist.

Margaret received the telegram telling of Lloyd's death. He was buried on Okinawa. Margaret cried and held Rodney for two days. The grief saturated not only Margaret but Leo and Edith as well. Their only living son was dead. Amy had lost her best friend and Evelyn had lost her idol. Edith was not sure she could go on, nor did she want to. Leo felt like his insides had been ripped out of him.

He and Lloyd had worked so well together. They seemed to know what the other one was thinking. Tasks were completed without the need for communication. Lloyd was the future of the ranch. There was a dark gloom over the entire place. There was no talking at the table during meals. Both Leo and Edith accomplished daily tasks mechanically.

Margaret not only mourned but worried about what she would do. She was living in a house owned by her dead husband's parents. She had no income and she had a son to raise by herself. Leo and Edith quickly resolved her concerns. "Margaret, we want you to live here with us. Don't worry about money for food or clothing. We'll provide for you and Rodney for as long as we live. You're family; and families take care of their own."

"Thank you. I do feel like I am a part of your family. And Rodney will always carry the Furman name."

Rodney was the one thing that anchored the family to the living world. He was a typical three-year-old boy, full of life and into everything. His actions and activities would bring all of them out of any depression that would be taking place at the time. Leo would keep reminding himself and Edith, "Life is for the living, we must go on to care for them."

Three months after the notification of Lloyd's death, Margaret received a letter from Ray Hayes telling about Lloyd's death and what a great guy he was. Ray said all the men thought very highly of Lloyd. This was a big help to a grieving family.

Allowing Leo and Edith to provide everything for her and her son bothered Margaret. "You two have been so good to me but I really feel that I should take the responsibility of providing for Rodney and myself."

"Margaret, don't feel that way. You and Rodney are all we have left of Lloyd."

"I know, but life needs to go on for both Rodney and me. You can have Rodney here as often as you like. I just think it is time I find a job and a place to live in town."

"You do what you feel you need to do. We'll help you however we can."

"Thank you. I hoped you'd understand." After Margaret moved into town, Rodney continued to return to the ranch for the summers and on most weekends. Years later when the government decided to move the cemetery on Okinawa, Lloyd's body was sent to Rushville for burial in the family plot. There finally was closure for the family.

After the war ended, Hank Rath started working for Leo, and Amy was pregnant. Their first child, Leo Wayne, was born on April 21, 1946. Now Leo and Edith had two grandsons. Leo approached Hank about moving to the ranch. "Hank, I'm in need of help and you and Amy need help to getting started in married life. Why don't you move into the house that Lloyd and Margaret lived in and work for me?"

"I appreciate the offer but I want to be independent and build a place of our own."

"I understand that. You can have your independence and still move to our place. I'm not talking about just being a hired hand. Tell you what; every other year you put your brand on all the heifer calves. In three years you'll have the beginnings of a herd of your own."

"That sounds good except for the first three years or maybe four."

"Alright for four years you can have the profit for one fifth of the steers sold."

"Agreed. I know Amy will be pleased." Hank and Amy moved into the little house across the garden from Leo and Edith.

Rodney thought there was no one like his Grandpa and he wanted to be just like him, even to the point that he found a pair of scissors which he used to cut all the hair off the top of his head so he could be bald like Leo. "Rodney, why on earth did you cut off the hair on the top of your head?"

"Cause I wanted to look like Grandpa."

At Christmastime in 1946 Evelyn rode the bus home for the holidays. When she arrived in Rushville, she called for her Mom or Dad to come to town to pick her up. "I'm so glad you're home for Christmas. Unfortunately, your father has gone to a bull sale and won't be back until tomorrow. I can't get to town to get you right now. Why don't you stay with Margaret tonight and we'll pick you up in the morning."

"Alright, Mother, since this Saturday night there will be a dance in town and I'll go to that. It'll be a good chance to see a lot of friends."

At the dance August Vincent asked Evelyn to dance several times. "I danced with you once; not now, maybe later."

Three dances later, "How about this dance. You're a good dancer and I would very much like to dance more than once with you."

"Alright, you're not bad yourself." After some conversation, August asked, "May I take you home?"

"I don't know you very well and besides home is 12 miles southeast of town."

"I'd be happy to drive you out to where you live. And I'm a very trustworthy fellow. Ask anybody."

"Well, I'd like to go home rather than stay with my sister-in-law. I haven't seen my parents in a while."

"Good, we'll leave whenever you're ready."

"I'll need to go by my sister-in-law's apartment first and get my suitcase." August drove to Margaret's apartment and went in to be introduced and for Evelyn to tell Margaret that she was going on out to the ranch. When they left Margaret's, August's car was gone. "What happened?" Evelyn asked.

"I don't know. Someone must be playing a trick on me. Let's walk around the corner and see if they just moved my car." Evelyn felt like very person in Rushville was watching her walk down the street with her suitcase in hand and with a man she had only met. She was about to turn around and go back to Margaret's apartment when August's brother drove up in August's car.

"Just who do you think you are, taking my car, and where have you been?"

"I just borrowed it to take my girl, Sue, home. I came right back. I didn't think you'd even notice it being gone."

"Well, I did. We'll talk about this later. Right now we're going to take Evelyn out to her folk's place, so get in the back seat." That night a new romance began. On December 1, 1947, August and Evelyn were married.

In 1947 Edith got a new appliance, a freezer. The day after it was delivered she put Leo and Amy to work killing and cleaning chickens. Later in the fall she finished filling it with vegetables from the garden and freshly butchered beef. She thought the freezer was the greatest improvement ever. "No more canning beef and vegetables, unless I want to," she said to herself.

Margaret had recovered from Lloyd's death by 1947. In August she married Stanley Wright.

CHAPTER 11

A TIME TO KEEP AND A TIME TO THROW AWAY

There had been no additional purchased land added to the Furman ranch since James died. The ranch was well established. Then in the late 1940's Chris Abbott moved into Sheridan County and began buying land. He bought the Modisett place, plus the Selder and Tin-nin ranches. When he approached Leo about selling, Leo said no. Later he approached Leo about trading some land. "I'm not sure I want to trade any land, Chris. We're satisfied with the land we have now."

"Leo, I sure would like to own the southwest corner section of your place. I'd like to trade you three quarters of the section west of you for three quarters of the section in your southwest corner." After two days of deliberation Leo agreed to the trade. There would be no more changes to the ranch during Leo's lifetime.

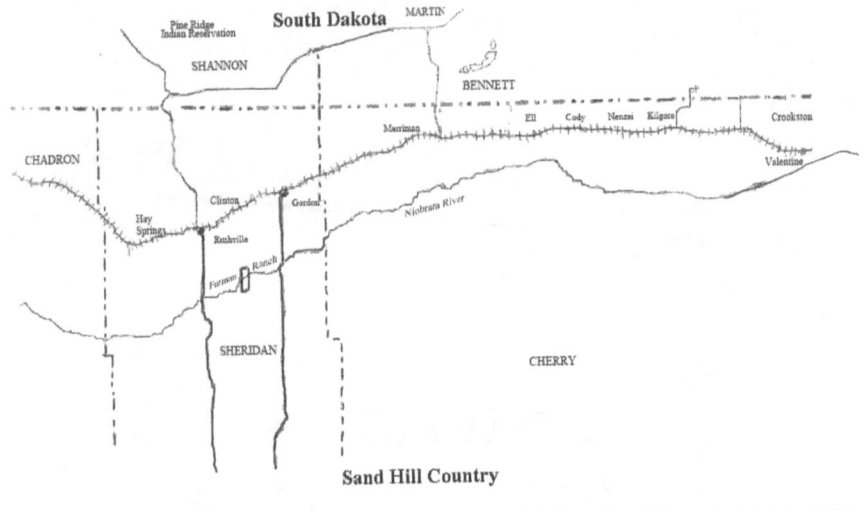

Sand Hill Country

Ranch Location

On November 18, 1948 a snowstorm began. It not only snowed and snowed, but the winds blew 50 to 70 miles per hour. Drifting closed all the roads. It was several days before travel resumed. The snow stayed on the ground until after Christmas. On the first day of January Leo went into Rushville to meet the west bound train. There were four bulls on the train that he had purchased in Iowa. While he was waiting on the train, he saw Evelyn and August walking toward the movie theater. "You two out to celebrate the New Year?"

"Yes, we're going to see 'The Green Grass of Wyoming'. Do you want to go with us?"

"No, thanks, I'm waiting for the train. The new bulls I bought are on it and I'm anxious to check on them." Leo went back to the station and waited. Later, snow started to fall. Leo continued to wait. Not only was the train late, it never came. The snowfall became heavier and the wind speed increased. Drifting snow was causing problems. Leo was stranded in town. He managed to drive over to Margaret and Stanley Wright's house to wait out the storm. He thought to himself, "I sure hope Evelyn and August got home before all this hit."

Vehicles were unable to move. The telephone lines went down. There could be no communications. There was nothing that could be done. The blizzard once again had 50 to 70mph winds and snow that fell for three days. Edith, Amy and Hank were isolated. When the snow stopped falling, Hank dug for a full day to make a path from his house to Edith and Leo's house, and then to the barn. Hank asked Edith, "Do you need some wood for the stove?"

"Yes, I do. I was able to bring in what was stacked by the back door, but that is gone now."

"I'll bring in plenty. Have you heard from Leo?"

"No I haven't. The phone lines must be down; I can't call anyone. I do hope he never started home."

Leo stayed the three days at Margaret's house. On the fourth day a bulldozer started clearing the town streets. But there was no way Leo could drive his pickup truck back to the ranch. Leo was anxious to get home. He was worried about Edith and the cattle.

Stanley suggested, "Why don't you call Pete Staub. He has a Piper Cub. Maybe he would fly you out to the ranch." Leo drove to Pete's house on the edge of town and asked, "Would you fly me out to our place. I'll pay you for your time and trouble."

"I'm willing to try if we can get the snow out of the way so I can take off. But landing might be impossible unless there is a bare spot some place where I could land."

"There's a hilltop south of the house that might be clear. Snow usually blows off into the lowlands."

"Then let's see if we can clear a lane with my Ford tractor. With the small blade that's on it, the snow may be too deep for us to move."

For half a day the two men dug, shoveled, and pushed snow. They finally cleared a long enough path for the plane to take off. The takeoff was uneventful. When they reached the river, Leo pointed, "There south of the house; see that plateau?"

"Yes, I see it….the snow doesn't look deep, but if it is, we're in trouble. The plane could go over on its nose when we land." Pete circled twice then decided to try a landing. The landing was not the smoothest, but there was no crash.

Edith was so happy to see Leo. "I didn't know what to think when I saw that plane come down. I was so worried about you. I didn't know if you were safe or frozen in a snowdrift someplace."

"I'm fine. I stayed with Margaret and Stanley the whole time. This is Pete Staub; he owns the plane."

"Thank you, Pete, for bringing Leo home."

"Glad I could help out. I'd like to stay and visit for awhile, but I want to get back before dark."

"Can I go back with you?"

"Edith, what are you saying?"

"I'm saying I've not been to town for more than two months and I've been inside the house for four days. I want to go to town. If Pete will take me, I'll put some clothes in a suitcase and go. I can stay with Margaret or Milla DeWitt until you can come and get me."

"My plane wasn't built to haul very much, but if you want to go back, pack your clothes and I'll take you. To Leo's surprise, Edith did. She bundled up and kissed Leo goodbye. Pete carried her suitcase out to the plane and Edith climbed into the back seat of the little Cub. She had to hold the suitcase on her lap. Pete started the engine and taxied to the edge of the plateau, then stopped and turned off the engine.

Leo hustled out to where the plane stopped. Pete and Edith were getting out. Pete said, "With the two inches of snow still on the ground and another person, I can't get up enough speed to take off. I'm not sure I can do it with just me in the plane." Edith and Leo watched as Pete climbed back in, revved up the engine and released the brakes. The plane moved forward slowly at first, then began to pick up speed. The tail finally raised and the plane began to lift off just as it reached the edge of the plateau. Pete was airborne.

There was so much snow everywhere, and deep drifts were in every valley. There was no way they were going to be able to take hay to all the cattle. "I am worried about the cattle. They can't find anything to eat in all this snow", Leo said to Hank. From the radio they learned that the National Guard and some Air Force units were dropping hay to stranded cattle.

When the phone service started again, Leo received a call informing him that the bulls had been offloaded at Valentine and were safe. If no more snow fell, they would be loaded back on a train and should arrive in Rushville in another day. Now that the phone was working again, Leo called for a hay drop for his cattle. He was told he would be put on the list, but there was no promise of help.

After three days of hard work and struggles, Leo, Edith, Hank and Amy were able to get hay to the closest cattle. While they were returning to the house, they heard a plane coming. Amy was the first to see it. "Look how low that plane is; it has got to be bringing hay."

Leo turned the horses toward the area where the other cattle should be, then the four of them stood in front of the horses to form an arrow point just as the plane flew over. Hank said, "Do you think they understood what we were trying to do?"

"I hope so, Hank."

It would be another nine days before they knew if the message was understood and resulted in their cattle receiving food. Hay had been dropped to the cattle but it had all been eaten by the time Leo and Hank finally got to them.

Leo received a phone call informing him that the bulls had arrived. He called Larry DeWitt and asked him to look after them for a couple of days. The new bulls stayed in the pens at the railroad yard and Larry DeWitt made sure they had hay until Leo could come after them.

In March another blizzard hit, but it was not as severe. The winter of 1948-49 turned out to be the worst since 1888. Leo and Hank only lost 20 head of cattle that winter. Others had lost much more livestock.

In June of 1950 North Korea attacked South Korea and the United States was involved in a war again. Only this time it was not called a war; still men were dying in a far away land. No Nebraska Furman men would be in service this time. As with other wars, the demand for food and beef increased. Steers sold in the next three fall sales yielded a good income.

By 1950 Hank and Amy were becoming more involved in operations on the ranch. Amy worked right alongside Hank during branding and haying times. Amy had many qualities of her parents. It was not uncommon for her to take milk, butter and eggs to elderly folks. In the future as she raised children, she would teach them about horses and nature. She also wanted them to know about the Lord. Since they didn't make it to town very often for church services, she would tell them Bible stories.

Leo was still very active in day-to-day operations, especially where the cattle were concerned. He was always proud of their Angus cattle. He searched for and bought bulls with good bloodlines so the quality of their herd would improve. He became very active in Nebraska's Angus Association. The Angus Association would sponsor tours in different parts of the state prior to the fall cattle sales. Whenever the tours were in the northwest part of the state, a stop at the Furman ranch was included.

The tour advertisement usually read: *This is an excellent opportunity for livestock people to visit and see some of the black breed's outstanding cattle. The association extends an invitation to all to attend and participate in this very educational and informative event.* On the day of cattle sales in Rushville, Leo's calves always topped the market.

Leo helped young men get started in raising Black Angus cattle. He introduced August to the Black Angus breed and helped him build up an Angus herd. When Lloyd's buddy, Ray Hayes, returned home from the Army, Leo helped him in buying a place in southern Nebraska and starting an Angus herd.

In the summer of 1951 the REA reached the ranch. There was a celebration and a prayer of thanks. There was electricity in both houses and in the barn. Edith said to Leo, "I feel like all the comforts of civilization have finally reached us." Leo gave their wind charger to August and Evelyn. It would be another three years before they would receive power from REA.

"Think of what we've seen in our lifetime, Edith. Not only the electric power, but the phone and motorized vehicles."

"You think of those things, but I think about the electric cooking stove, the washing machine, the electric iron, and the refrigerator."

"What about the day we saw the airplane bring hay to our cattle. When I was a boy there was no thought given to people flying."

"Yes, we have seen a lot of changes in our lifetime."

When Rodney was 10 he tested his roping abilities by roping one of the barn cats. Barn cats are nothing like a pet household cat, and this one took offense at a rope around its neck. So off it ran and up the nearest tree. Rodney went complaining into the house, "Grandma, the old gray cat ran off with my rope and I want it back!"

Edith saw Hank out at the barn and asked him to intercede. Hank found the cat with the rope still around its neck, clinging to some high tree limbs. He climbed the tree, which surprised both Rodney and the cat. It wanted no part in anything human. It became a spitting, scratching, biting wildcat.

Hank returned to the ground and went into the barn for a pole that had a hook on the end. Again he climbed the tree and hooked the rope, then lowered the cat and himself to the ground. With the hook he was able to separate the cat from the rope. He returned the rope to Rodney. He thought he would hear a "thank you". Instead he heard, "How can an old man like you climb a tree?" Hank just grinned, "I'm only 30, Rodney."

The Furman's felt blessed during those early 1950's years. Raising cattle was prosperous and weather conditions were favorable until the mid-1950's when a drought came. Then, crops dried up and there was very little grass. Fortunately it did not last as long as the 30's drought.

Amy and Hank were blessed by the birth of a daughter, Amy Jo, in June of 1952. Two years later in March of 1954, Evan Ted was born. In another two years, Edith Ann was born in May. Leo and Edith felt so blessed by having five grandchildren. The hurtful loss of their own children was lessened now but would never be forgotten. Two more boys would be born before the end of 1960.

As the children grew, they were allowed to play with Leo's hat and boots. Rodney had been allowed the same privilege as he grew up. A bemused Amy would say, "Dad, you never let Lloyd or me even touch your hat or boots, now these kids put them on all the time."

"Well, life has taught me that hats and boots are not as special as I thought they were."

The Rath children grew up on the ranch. They learned to do chores just as their mother and grandparents had. They played the same way their mother and their uncle, Lloyd, had played.

One Wednesday morning when Larry DeWitt was taking fuel to the ranch, his wife, Milla, and their two children went with him. Edith cooked a big dinner and the DeWitt's stayed to eat and visit. Later Edith played the piano and sang several songs. Milla, Kathleen, and Lawrence would join in from time to time. Larry and Leo usually just listened.

Sadly disaster returned in 1956. Hank and Amy's oldest son, Leo Wayne, and his cousin, who had come for a visit before school started, were playing outside. The day was warm and the leaves were falling. Edith asked the two boys to help rake the leaves in the yard and drag them to the hillside to be burned.

The boys were making a game of it, but Edith soon got tired and went into the house to rest. The boys continued to rake for a short while. Then they decided the leaf pile was big enough and was ready to be burned. They got matches and a bucket which they partially filled with kerosene. As Leo Wayne carried the bucket, some of the kerosene splashed on his pants and shoes. The fire was lit and quickly flamed up.

The two boys realized their mistake and tried to stamp out the fire. Young Leo's pants caught fire and he ran for the house. Edith heard the yelling and looked out the kitchen window. Seeing Leo burning, she grabbed a rag rug she was making and ran out the door. She wrapped him in the rug and rolled him on the ground. When the fire on Leo Wayne was out, she carried him into the house. With tears in her eyes, she put towels soaked with water on him and telephoned the doctor for help.

Hank and Amy had gone to town for groceries. They were on their way back when the fire truck and the doctor went rushing past them. They realized something was terribly wrong and joined the race to the ranch. Milla's husband, Larry, was the fire chief in Rushville. He had a great concern for what had happened. The doctor said, "The boy is badly burned and needs to be in a hospital immediately."

Larry said, "Sam Gouding has an airplane and I know he'll help."

"So call him," Amy and Hank almost said together. Larry called and within an hour a four passenger Cessna landed south of the house. The doctor had coated the boy with Vaseline and wrapped him in gauze. Gently they carried Leo to the plane and loosely fastened him in. Amy and Hank crammed in as well. The plane left for the hospital in Denver. Young Leo Wayne died before they reached Denver. He was 10 years old.

The Niobrara almost reached flood stage from the tears shed on the Furman ranch. No one was untouched, especially Edith. "How many boys will I see die? Why them?" Amy now felt the same pain her mother had felt four times before.

The manliness in both Leo and Hank broke down. They cried as much as the two mothers. Leo repeated what he had said too many times before, "We have got to go on for the living."

Winter brought a blizzard to sand hill country again. It was not as bad as the one seven years ago, but it was a difficult time. The ranch was isolated from the rest of the world because of drifted snow. The telephone provided a communication link to Rushville and the news and weather were heard from the radio. A week went by before a road to town opened for travel. Leo felt fortunate that no cattle were lost.

That spring they planted 30 acres of corn near the old blockhouse. The plot was on high sandy ground and there was little rain that summer. The corn only grew to a three foot height, but the sand burrs did much better. In the fall the snows came early and covered both the corn stalks and the sand burrs. When Rodney came out for a weekend, Leo asked him, "Rodney, would you take a team and a wagon and pick some of the corn we planted?"

"Sure, Grandpa."

"You will not get many ears but what you get we can use for animal feed."

Rodney found picking the corn was no easy task. He either had to stoop over or crawl on his hands and knees to find the corn in the snow. He soon was covered in sand burrs. Pulling off and fighting the burrs got worse and worse; however, Rodney did manage to pick enough corn to fill most of the wagon. He drove back to the barn full of disdain and frustration. He walked up to Leo and said, "I'm tired of fighting sand burrs. If you want that corn picked, then you pick it!"

"Calm down, Rodney. I didn't know it was going to be that bad. Maybe we should just leave the corn for the birds and animals". When Monday came, Hank and Leo moved some cattle into the corn patch.

In the winter of 1958-59, the brood cows were moved into the trees north of the river and west of the house. There was a calving shed there that was used to shelter early spring calves. In late February Hank and Rodney were trying to get a cow and her newborn calf into the shed. The cow had other ideas and gave them a lot of trouble, so they maneuvered her into the corral. They thought they would give the cow time to calm down, and then move her into the shed. Leo arrived about that time. "What's going on?"

"We're waiting for this cow to quiet down so we can get her into the shed."

"She and that calf need to be in there now as cold as it is. I'll see if I can drive her into the shed."

"She's pretty wild, Grandpa."

Leo climbed over the corral fence and said, "When I get her near the gate, open it and stand in front of the trees." The cow felt threatened and charged Leo. Leo quickly reached the top of the corral fence.

"Grandpa, I didn't know you could move that fast."

"I do believe she would take a man down."

An hour later they were able to move the cow and calf into the shed. The shed had saved a lot of calves over the years.

In the summer of 1959 Leo and Edith decided it was time for them to move into town. Edith was beginning to feel her age. Leo would go back out to the ranch every day after they moved. Amy and Hank moved into their ranch house after they left. The first change they made was to install an oil furnace. Edith and Leo had always used a wood-burning stove to heat the house.

Rodney moved into Edith and Leo's town home for his last year of high school. He graduated in 1960. After graduation he thought he would try college. He enrolled in the University of Wyoming, but dropped out after one year. Then Rodney worked for his step-father in a grocery store in Rushville and continued to work some on the ranch, especially in summers during hay time.

The prices paid for steers began falling after the Korean War ended and during the 1960's they reached a very low level. Although income was reduced, there were no financial problems.

Another change during the transition from the 50's to the 60's concerned the task of branding. Branding was becoming less of a task and more of a contest and social event.

People would gather at the ranch doing the branding. The work was still done, the iron applied, castrations, vaccinations, and earmarking. But there were now contests in cutting (separating a steer from the rest of the herd) and roping and wrestling calves down. The women would prepare a big meal and when the work was done, card playing would take place.

CHAPTER 12
A TIME TO DIE

In the 1960's the political thinking in the United States changed. It was an era of controversy. Ideas and actions vacillated from one extreme to another. The public's focus was on….. "me" and "we". In the midst of the confusion another military action mushroomed in a place called Viet Nam. It began with America sending "advisers" into the country. By August of 1965 there were 125,000 American solders in Viet Nam. Local draft boards became active inducting thousands of men into service.

Rodney was drafted in June of 1964. After he completed basic training he was assigned to the 5th Army in Ft. Riley. When the 5th Army was transferred to Viet Nam, Rodney was assigned stateside duty because he was a sole-surviving son. He was discharged two years later. The war continued until 1975. Sadly, the American public never supported the war effort, or the men who served.

Rodney returned to Rushville and tried to start life where he left it two years earlier. He had made new friends but his time in the army had not been memorable. He had trouble deciding what to do, going from one thing to another. The one thing that did hold him firm was going out to the ranch and working for his Grandpa.

In the spring of 1969 Hank and Amy's daughter, Amy Jo, had gone into Rushville to decorate the high school gym for the prom. It was a fun afternoon hanging balloons and crepe paper streamers. When they finished, she told a friend, "I'm going to call Mom and tell her I am stopping to buy shampoo and lipstick before I start home."

She dialed the phone and after seven or eight rings, her brother, Gene, answered. "Gene, tell Mom I want to stop at the drugstore before I go home."

"Ok, I'll tell her. I think she's asleep on the couch." He went into the living room and softly said, "Mom". Then louder, "Mom". He touched her and she did not move. Gene was frightened and immediately went looking for his father. "Dad, come quick! Something's wrong with Mom. I can't wake her up." Hank ran to the house. He checked for a heartbeat, but felt none.

"Gene, call the doctor. Tell him to hurry!" The doctor came right away. After a quick examination, he turned to Hank and said, "Hank, I'm sorry.... She's dead."

"No! You must be wrong!"

"I'm sorry Hank. I think she must have had a heart attack." Amy had died in her sleep. She was 48 years old. Amy Jo never went to the prom but did attend her graduation ceremony. Nothing seemed the same after her Mother, Amy died. Amy Jo took her mother's place for the rest of her family.

In 1970 Rodney had a date with a girl in Rushville. When he got to her apartment she was not there. Her roommate, Mariann answered the door. She was babysitting a neighbor girl. "She's not here; surely she didn't forget your date. She should be home soon. You're welcome to come in and wait for her if you want."

"I might as well since I'm here." Rodney and Mariann watched television and talked. The next time Rodney went back, it was to see Mariann. The two of them were married December 10, 1970.

Work on the ranch remained the same. Branding took place in the spring, the cattle were moved to pasture in May, grass was cut for hay in the summer, and the cattle were moved closer to the river for winter and those slated for market were separated. There were fences to be repaired and cattle that needed to be doctored from time to time. Leo, Hank, and Rodney always had plenty to do and extra help was hired when needed.

The world beyond the sand hills did not seem to influence the Rushville area until 1973. Newspaper headlines told of the Sioux Indians capturing Federal State law enforcement personnel. The location was Wounded Knee, South Dakota, the same place where the U.S. Calvary slaughtered 300 Indians 82 years earlier. The American Indian Movement activists wanted more self-government. They armed themselves and kept law enforcement at bay. The confrontation lasted 70 days before civil order was restored.

While this was going on, Edith began suffering from back pain. After two months. Leo told her, "You need to see a doctor."

"I'll be alright. I think it's just arthritis." A month later the pain was worse and she agreed to see a doctor. The doctor sent her to the Gordon hospital for tests. She remained in the hospital for three days. Leo was with her when the doctor said, "You have a cancerous tumor on your kidney and it needs to be removed. After it's removed, you should have relief and be able to have a normal life."

"At my age I don't know if I want to have surgery or not. What do you think, Leo?"

"I think you should. Cancer is very serious and needs to be dealt with immediately. But you do what you think best."

Edith wanted to go home and think about it. Evelyn drove both back to Rushville. On the way Edith asked, "Evelyn, do you think I'm too old for surgery?"

"Why, no, Mother, I think you should have the surgery as soon as possible. It could get worse if you don't do anything. The doctor said you should feel better after surgery."

The surgery was scheduled for October 9th, Edith's birthday, at the Rushville hospital. The surgeon soon discovered there were more tumors than he could remove. He just closed the incision. Edith recovered from the surgery but suffered from cancer for 11 weeks.

During those last weeks Leo stayed close to Edith. He didn't go to the ranch. They knew the future for Edith was very short. They talked about good memories and a few bad ones. "Leo, the day you came to move me from my aunt's to your father's ranch, I wondered what am I getting into? I was scared. Yet I didn't think I had much choice."

"You know what I remember about that day?"

"No."

"All the way back, I kept trying to look out of the corner of my eye at you. I was thinking you were the prettiest girl that I had ever seen and I couldn't think of anything to say."

"Is that why I had to do all the talking?" They both laughed.

Edith talked about the changes she saw in their world. "The town is shrinking. The young people are moving away."

Leo agreed, "There are fewer farms and ranches, too. The big outfits are buying the little ones out. It's not just the young people that are gone. There are fewer people in the area."

"I thought the other day when I was in the grocery store about all the businesses that had closed up. Why if I wanted to buy a new dress, I'd have to go to Chadron or buy it from a catalog. I used to buy clothes right here in Rushville."

"Our world is changing. I'm not sure for the better, but it's changing. I think about how the river has changed. As I was growing up, the river was wider and deeper. It never was real deep, but there were places where you could swim. Even our kids swam in some of the deep pockets. Now look at it. In the summer it almost dries completely up."

"I've noticed that too, Leo. Why do you think that has happened? Do we get that much less rainfall?"

"No, I don't think so. The real cause is all the irrigation that has gone on over the years and the dams that were built. For years there has been a lot of water taken from the riverbed to water hay meadows around here. Then on the east side of the state where there is a lot of farming, they started installing center pivot irrigation systems with deep wells 10 to 15 years ago. That brought the ground water to the surface. But it lowered the water table. There has been a lot of water taken from the riverbed for crops and hay meadows."

"I remember when the bridge was out and we had to wade the river, putting our shoes high enough on the bank so they wouldn't fall into the river."

"Well, the bridge is high enough now that I don't think it will ever wash out."

"Leo, I feel like the river must feel."

"What do you mean?"

"I feel tired and used up."

"Don't feel like that Edith. Why don't you rest now?"

Edith died on January 1, 1974. Leo felt lost and alone. They had been married 59 years. He found it almost impossible to follow his philosophy of…we have got to keep going for the living.

Leo struggled. He continued on for a few years, and then Alzheimer's began to take control of his life. The man that had been so vibrant now relied on others. Leo died on October 18, 1980. His obituary read in part:

> *Leo Furman was a rancher. He was America riding a horse, democracy wearing a big hat, freedom holding a branding iron. He wrestled the range for a living and squeezed life from the sand hills of Nebraska.*
>
> *Leo liked the smell of hay and the aroma of good leather. He liked the reflection of the sunrise on the Niobrara River as the day's chores began and its peaceful steadfast flow as the sun cast its evening shadows across the ranch. He liked the sound of cattle and seemed to understand them. Cattle were his life, he was a rancher.*
>
> *The wind brought life and death to the ranch. It brought welcome rain, terrible storms and gentle breezes. The peaceful sound of the windmill on the hill was a favorite sound of his.*
>
> *He was a strong and gentle man. Strong enough to break a horse, rope a steer and gentle enough to place a newborn calf on its feet for the first time.*

His son fought in World War II. His daughters brought gentleness to the ranch, his wife stood with him through the good years as well as the hard ones.

He liked buckwheat cakes, strong coffee, biscuits and homemade ice cream. He liked big hats, good boots and fast horses.

He, like all ranchers, lived by the code of the sand hills and never refused a helping hand to friend or stranger.

This was a very fitting description of who Leo Furman was and what the Furman ranch was about. Leo is gone and an era has closed. What had been built by a father and son would end. The land is still there as well as the river. The grass still waves in a breeze, the river still flows eastward, and peacefulness still hovers over the land.

The ranch was divided into three parts. The three new owners of the ranch are Leo's daughter, Evelyn Vincent; his grandson, Rodney Furman; and the living children of Hank and Amy Rath.

As a young boy I called Leo "my other Grandpa." In reality he was my great uncle.

> **"Nothing but memories as we journey on,**
>   **Longing for a smile from loved ones gone.**
>   **Thoughts return to scenes now past;**
>   **Time rolls on, but memories last."**
> Anonymous